23545

LD
353
.W5

White
History of Baylor University
1845-1861

History of Baylor University 1845 - 1861

By

MICHAEL A. WHITE

Library of Congress Catalog Card Number
68 - 29764

Published by

P. O. Box 1684
Waco, Texas

Binding by
Library Binding Co.
Waco, Texas

To my wife, Anita

Introduction

With the approach of the centennial of Baylor University in 1945, it was decided that a history of Baylor should be written. At first projected as a pictorial history, the plan was changed to provide a thorough coverage of the subject. Nothing short of a really monumental work could do proper credit to this great institution—"a voice in the wilderness"—from 1845.

A large amount of spade work in the form of research and writing was necessary. Therefore, the Texas Collection and the History Department of Baylor University, in collaboration, assigned to mature and able students for masters theses, eras, personalities, institutions, etc. in the life of Baylor. With this work as a basis of further research and writing, by the commissioned author, we are producing the planned major work in two volumes, Baylor University, 1845-1886, and Baylor University, 1886-1945.

Michael Allen White came to the Texas Collection as my assistant in 1955 and remained either continuously or by summers through 1967. As a result of his deep knowledge of the collection and of the history of Baylor, one of the first project theses—*Baylor University, 1845-1861*—was assigned to him. He worked hard and fruitfully on it. The work was completed and approved and was partial fulfillment of the requirements of the Master of Arts degree.

Since graduation he has taught successfully, been a Peace Corps worker in Liberia, is at present a teacher of history at McLennan Community College, and is currently enrolled in the Ed.D. program at Baylor.

This book, the published version of his thesis, is a brief, interesting, and enlightening story of those first years.

Guy Bryan Harrison
Professor of History
Director of Texas Collection
Baylor University
Waco, Texas

Acknowledgments

The writer acknowledges his deep obligation to Professor Guy B. Harrison for his invaluable aid and encouragement, and for making available the materials in the archives of the Texas Collection of Baylor University, and to Dr. E. Bruce Thompson for his advice in the many technical aspects of the original manuscript.

Table of Contents

List of Illustrations

1

The Beginning

THE BAYLOR University of today with its large campus, its numerous buildings, its hundreds of teachers and thousands of students came into being through the efforts of a few enlightened individuals. These pioneers of education endeavored to create an institution of learning which would not only benefit their denomination but the people of Texas as well. The Baylor University of today stands as a monument to their success. These humble but determined few faced many hardships and obstacles before achieving their dream. Many of the people of Texas, as did most of the common people in the United States, looked upon education with disfavor and distrust.[1] Even the Baptists in Texas for whose enlightenment the school was established would not give the support so desperately needed in the early years. Many times the trustees and a few other faithful supporters of the dream delved into their own scantily supplied pockets.[2] In spite of the financial difficulties and lack of moral support, Baylor University continued to function during the trying years of its infancy. Credit for this fact must go to those few Baptist pioneers of education who were willing to sacrifice much for the welfare and enlightenment of future generations.

By the early 1800's there were various Baptist groups throughout the United States, especially in the South, and especially among the common folk. When Stephen F. Austin settled his original three hundred colonists, there were eleven known Baptist families in the group.[3] Among these families were John McNeese, his wife Ivey and a family named Allcorn.[4]

---

[1]J. B. Link (ed.), **Texas Historical and Biographical Magazine** (Austin, 1891), Vol. I, 468.
[2]J. M. Carroll, **A History of Texas Baptists** (Dallas: Baptist Standard Publishing Company, 1923), p. 231.
[3]**Ibid.,** p. 29.
[4]Worth S. Ray, **Austin Colony Pioneers** (Austin, 1949), pp. 1, 10.

Prior to the Texas Revolution the only legal religion in Texas was the Roman Catholic Church. Article three of the Mexican Constitution of 1824 stated that "the religion of the Mexican nation is and will be perpetually the Roman Catholic Apostolic."[5] Baptists, however, were of that nature that would not be easily deterred from whatever they believed to be the true faith. This law, therefore, did not stop Baptist activities in Texas. As early as 1824, the Reverend Freeman Smally, a Baptist missionary from Ohio, preached at Pecan Point on the Texas side of the Red River. In the home of one William Newman he preached the first sermon by a Baptist in Texas.[6] In 1825 Reverend Joseph Bays preached the first Baptist sermon on the west side of the Brazos River—at San Felipe in the home of Moses Shipman. Reverend Thomas Hanks came from Tennessee in 1829 and for a time lived in the home of this same Moses Shipman, the "Aquila of Texas Baptists." Under Hanks' preaching the first recorded profession of faith was made in Texas, that of Mrs. Lydia Allcorn.[7]

Since Roman Catholicism was alien to many of the colonists, families would gather for devotions in their own homes. Soon others would come and join these "services," but no churches as such could be organized because of the law.[8] In the 1820's there were at least twenty Baptist preachers in Texas, and at least three Sunday Schools and one regular prayer meeting were organized in spite of the law.[9]

In the 1830's other Baptist preachers came to Texas, and several churches were organized. In 1834 Reverend Samuel Reed came from Tennessee and preached in the Nacogdoches area. Services were first held in secret, but by 1836 the meetings were being held openly. Reverend Abner Smith, an Anti-Missionary Baptist, came to Texas with a colony of thirty-two, the entire membership of his church in Alabama. This church was active for only a few years.[10] In 1838 Reverend Daniel Parker organized a church in Illinois and with the entire membership migrated to Texas.[11]

The first regular Missionary Baptist church organized

---

[5]Carroll, **Texas Baptists**, p. 8.
[6]B. F. Riley, **History of the Baptists of Texas** (Dallas: B. F. Riley, 1907), pp. 14-17.
[7]**Ibid.**, pp. 14-17.
[8]**Ibid.**, p. 20.
[9]Carroll, **Texas Baptists**, p. 17.
[10]Riley, **Baptists of Texas**, p. 17.
[11]Carroll, **Texas Baptists**, p. 18.

in Texas was established through the efforts of Reverend Z. N. Morrell at Washington-on-the-Brazos in 1837.[12] This church had at the beginning only six members and soon went out of existence. In 1839 Reverend Thomas Spraggins came from Mississippi to visit his son at Independence and stayed long enough to organize a Baptist church.[13] Many other Baptist churches were organized in the 1830's, and the denomination grew steadily from that time on.[14]

Although there were a goodly number of Baptist in Texas by the late 1830's, they were anything but united in doctrine or practices. In 1839 delegates from the small and scattered churches in the western settlements met in Independence to form an association. Holding true to the sincere but often obstinate Baptist spirit, dissention almost immediately appeared. Through the efforts of R. E. B. Baylor, who had come to Texas earlier that year, Reverend Abner Smith was chosen as moderator. One Reverend T. W. Cox expressed violent opposition to Smith's selection because Smith was a conservative, while Cox considered himself a liberal. After working three or four days toward agreement upon an abstract of principles by which the association could be formed, little progress was made due to Smith's obstinancy. Finally through the prayers and entreaties of Baylor and others, the old man yielded a little, and a platform of principles was drawn up. Just as it seemed that some sort of unity was accomplished, Reverend Cox got up and made a "warm and excited speech" which resulted in several of the delegates walking out of the meeting along with Cox. Thus ended the first attempt to organize a Baptist association in Texas.[15]

On October 8, 1840, delegates from three Baptist chuurches met in the town of Travis and organized the Baptist Union Association.[16] This association was composed of churches from Travis, La Grange, and Independence; three ministers: T. W. Cox, R. E. B. Baylor, and I. L. Davis; and fifty-three communicants. Baylor, now a circuit judge, was not a delegate to the

---

[12]Joseph Martin Dawson, **A Century with Texas Baptists** (Nashville: Broadman Press, 1947), p. 2.

[13]Ray, **Austin Colony**, p. 39.

[14]Carroll, **Texas Baptists**, p. 28.

[15]R. E. B. Baylor Manuscript concerning early Baptist work in Texas (Baylor Family Papers, Texas Collection, Baylor University. Hereafter cited as R. E. B. Baylor Manuscript).

[16]David Benedict, **A General History of the Baptist Denomination in America and Other Parts** (New York: Lewis Colby and Company, 1848), p. 786.

meeting because of judicial duties elsewhere. Reverend Cox acted as moderator of the organizational meeting, and an abstract of principles, more liberal than proposed at the first attempt, was quickly adopted.[17]

The Union Association grew steadily—by 1845 the association was comprised of 19 churches, 10 ministers, and 600 members. Two other associations had by that time been organized: the Sabine Association with 16 churches, 7 ministers, and 500 members; the Northern Association with 5 churches, 3 ministers, and 125 members.[18]

The Union Association was the largest and most active Baptist group in Texas. It was this association with its capable and learned leaders that formulated the idea of a Baptist literary institution. The first step was taken on October 7, 1841 during an associational meeting.[19] A committee composed of William H. Ewing, James Huckins, and a "Brother Green" presented a report concerning education: "Resolve that this association recommends the formation of an Educational Society, and that the brethren generally unite and endeavor to promote the objects of this society."[20] Because of the Mexican invasions of 1841 and 1842 the society was not organized until 1843.[21] R. E. B. Baylor was elected president; S. P. Andrews, recording secretary; William M. Tryon, corresponding secretary; a "Brother Collins," treasurer; James Huckins, Stephen Williams, William Ewing, J. S. Lester, J. L. Farquhar, Gail Borden, Z. N. Morrell, Board of Managers.[22]

Early in 1845 the society, mainly through the efforts of Baylor and Tryon, obtained from the Congress of the Republic of Texas the charter for a literary institution. Even after the establishment of the university the society remained active, devoting itself to the task of providing funds for the education of young ministers. The society paid the entire expenses of some ministerial students and the partial expenses of others according to the young men's financial condition.[23] Prior to 1886 at least

[17]R. E. B. Baylor Manuscript.
[18]Benedict, **History of the Baptist Denomination**, p. 786.
[19]Z. N. Morrell, **Fruits and Flowers from the Wilderness or 36 Years in Texas** (Boston: Gould and Lincoln, 1872), p. 216.
[20]Carroll, **Texas Baptists**, p. 228.
[21]**Ibid.**
[22]**Report on the Legal Relation of Baylor University to the Baptist State Convention of Texas** (Waco, 1859), p. 4.
[23]Morrell, **Fruits and Flowers**, p. 217.

nine-tenths of the ministerial students attending Baylor University were aided by the Education Society.[24]

Two men were largely responsible for the founding of Baylor University—R. E. B. Baylor and William M. Tryon. The Education Society was organized at Baylor's suggestion; the idea of a literary institution came from Tryon. Baylor contributed more money, but Tryon had more influence in the organization of the institution.[25]

William M. Tryon was born in New York State on March 10, 1809. At the age of seventeen he was converted and baptized. He was licensed to preach at Augusta, Georgia in 1832. Tryon studied for three years at Mercer University in Georgia. In 1841, at the request of Jesse Mercer, he was sent to Texas by the American Baptist Home Mission Society. Tryon settled near Washington-on-the-Brazos and became chaplain of the Texas Congress.[26] From 1841 to 1846 he was pastor of the Independence Church, one of the largest and most influential Baptist churches in Texas.[27] In 1846 he moved to Houston where he pastored a church which grew from a membership of seven to a congregation of over one hundred members.[28]

In 1841 Tryon attended his first session of the Union Association—it was at that session that the proposal was made to form the Education Society. As a member of the society Tryon suggested the establishment of a university.[29] Tryon was a born leader; he tirelessly worked for the establishment of the institution, and he, more than anyone, provided motivation and enthusiasm needed to carry out the dream for a Baptist university in Texas.

Tryon just did live long enough to see his dream become a reality—when in 1847 an epidemic of yellow fever broke out in Houston, that man of God, true to his Christian principles, chose to remain and minister to the sick. Tryon contracted the disease and died on November 16.[30] Baptists throughout Texas were saddened at the loss of one so respected and admired. The Board of Trustees of the university for which Tryon worked so hard to establish expressed sorrow and regret at losing one of the best supporters of education in Texas. Baylor University had sustained a "great loss in being deprived of the labors of

---

[24]Carroll, **Texas Baptists,** p. 175.
[25]**Ibid.,** p. 230.
[26]R. E. B. Baylor Manuscript.
[29]Link, **Historical and Biographical Magazine,** p. 191.
[30]Morrell, **Fruits and Flowers,** p. 136.

one who aided in bringing the institution into being, and who ever felt the livelist (*sic*) in its welfare."[31]

R. E. B. Baylor was born in Kentucky in 1791, and he received his education in a country school and an academy in Paris, Kentucky. He then studied law and by the age of twenty-three was a member of the Kentucky state legislature. In 1838 he moved to Alabama. While in Alabama the people of the Tuscaloosa District twice sent him to Congress. Baylor was converted, baptized, and licensed to preach in 1838 by the Talladega Baptist Church in Talladega County, Alabama. Baylor came to Texas in 1839, and he was equally successful in his new home, serving in the Texas Congress, in the Texas Supreme Court, and as Judge of the Circuit Court for fifteen years. Baylor was a conscientious Christian; he preached wherever he held court. He was an active participant in denominational work and had much influence among its leaders.[32]

Judge Baylor was a strong advocate of education; in fact, the first work he did in Texas was teaching.[33] The Education Society was formed at his suggestion, and he worked closely with Tryon toward the establishment of a university contributing money time and time again.[34] Baylor's greatest contribution to the denomination and to the university, however, was his respectability and his popularity with the people of Texas. His position as a judge as well as his popularity gave standing and respectability to the sometimes looked-down-upon Baptists and to their struggling little university.[35]

Once the university was actually established, other men played important roles in the affairs of Baylor University. Many of these men were ministers. Reverend Hosea Garrett was a member of the Education Society and, for many years, president of the Board of Trustees. Garrett first met with the Board as a proxy in 1847.[36] Hosea Garrett was absent from meeting of the Board only once in twenty years. He also acted as agent for the university from 1856 to 1866 and endeavored to carry out the thankless and difficult task of getting money for the support of the school from the not-too-eager or willing Baptists

[31]Copy of the Minutes of the Board of Trustees of Baylor University, June 3, 1848, p. 36 (Texas Collection, Baylor University. Hereafter cited as Minutes).

[32]Link, **Historical and Biographical Magazine**, p. 195.

[33]R. E. B. Baylor Manuscript.

[34]Carroll, **Texas Baptists**, pp. 212, 230.

[35]Link, **Historical and Biographical Magazine**, pp. 195-196.

[36]Minutes, May 1, 1847, p. 29.

of Texas. When there was work to be done, he was usually assigned to it, and the work was always done to the best of his ability.[37] It was, therefore, Hosea Garrett who came closest to filling the void left by Tryon's untimely death.

Reverend James Huckins did much to help the university in its early years. He was appointed the first agent to collect funds for buildings. Huckins travelled throughout Texas, Mississippi, Alabama, and perhaps some other states before he was able to raise funds sufficient for the erection of the first building of the new institution.[38]

Reverend J. W. D. Creath not only contributed his time as a member of the Board of Trustees, he also contributed $2,000 for the endowment of the Education Society and Baylor University. In his will Creath bequeathed his valuable theological library to the school.[39]

Several laymen were also outstanding in their support of the university. Among these were Albert Gallitan Haynes, A. C. Horton, and Judge A. S. Lipscomb. Albert G. Haynes was a Trustee. He came to Texas penniless but soon accumulated, by the standards of the day, a large fortune. He boarded students at his home and contributed considerable sums of money to the school.[40] Horton was another layman who contributed money during the early trials of the school. At one time he gave $5,000 which at that time was a princely sum.[41] Judge Lipscomb, a member of the first Texas Supreme Court, was an active Baptist and enthusiastic supporter of the university. A complete account of the men who participated in the advancement of the university in its early years is not possible, but the men who did give of their time and money were relatively few when compared with the many Baptists who were indifferent or unable to give support.

The Baptist denomination in the 1840's was trying very hard to obtain respectability among the people of Texas and the United States. Baptists were most numerous among that part of the population which had very little in the way of material wealth or educational achievement. Baylor University was

---

[37]Link, **Historical and Biographical Magazine**, pp. 468-469.

[38]R. E. B. Baylor Manuscript.

[39]Link, **Historical and Biographical Magazine**, p. 204.

[40]**Ibid.**, p. 376.

[41]J. J. Lane, **History of Education in Texas** (Washington: Government Printing Office, 1903), p. 70.

[42]Harry Haynes, "Dr. Rufus C. Burleson," **Southwestern Historical Review**, V (July, 1901), p. 53.

founded by educated and enlightened men dedicated to the task of raising the standards of their denomination. Several of the trustees held college degrees; others were self-educated. All realized the important place of education in the advancement of Baptists in Texas. In a letter to his brother Richard, Rufus Burleson, then President of Baylor University, said that there were "more learned men, classic scholars—regular graduates in this Union Association than in all North Alabama."[43] The early leaders of Texas were also educated, cultured men. According to one authority, no constitution of any government has been signed by so many well-educated men.[44] With so many educated leaders in the state, education would naturally have an important place in their thoughts and activities.

The desire on the part of Texas Baptists for a literary institution was not unique among the Baptists of that day. In the 1840's and earlier, Baptists in the South were actively establishing schools. Furman Academy was begun by South Carolina Baptists in the 1820's; by 1850 it had become a full-fledged university.[45] In North Carolina the Baptists founded Wake Forest College in 1834, Chowan Female Collegiate Institute in 1847, and Oxford Female College in 1851.[46] Georgia Baptists established Mercer Institute in 1833.[47] Also in 1833 the Alabama State Baptist Convention began a Manual Labor School.[48] In 1842 a classical school was started in Marion, and Judson Female College came under the control of the convention in 1843.[49] The Baptist leaders in Texas, being mostly from the South, were naturally influenced by the activities and educational philosophies of their compatriots elsewhere in the South. The idea of a coeducational schools, however, was not prevalent among Southern Baptists. Whereas they did establish separate male and female schools, there were no known coeducational institutions supported by the denomination. In fact, female education

---

[43]Letter from R. C. Burleson to Richard Burleson, February 6, 1854 (R. C. Burleson Papers, Texas Collection, Baylor University).

[44]Frederick Eby, **The Development of Education in Texas** (New York: The Macmillan Company, 1925), p. 80.

[45]Edgar J. Knight (ed.), **A Documentary History of Education in the South Before 1860,** Vol. IV (5 vols.; Chapel Hill: University of North Carolina Press, 1933), pp. 395-402.

[46]**Ibid.,** pp. 110, 401-402.

[47]**Ibid.,** p. 110.

[48]**Ibid.,** pp. 116-117.

[49]**Ibid.,** pp. 395-396.

was not even advocated by most Baptists in the South until the 1850's.[50]

Other denominations in Texas, especially the Methodists, were active in the establishment of schools. Rutersville College and McKenzie College were established in 1840. Wesleyan College was begun in 1844.[51] Secular groups were also busily starting schools in the Republic during the 1840's. The University of Nacogdoches was founded in 1845; Marshall University in 1842; and Galveston University in 1840.[52] This period did indeed seem to be an auspicious time for beginning a Baptist literary institution in Texas.

The founders of the school were beset with many problems from the very beginning. Texas in 1845, in spite of the growing interest in education, was at best an unlikely place to begin an institution of higher learning. Although American settlement had begun in 1821, Texas was still very much a frontier. There were no railroads; communication was almost non-existent; and the few roads were merely animal or Indian trails.[53] Many Indians, supposedly friendly, roamed freely about Texas stealing, murdering, and plundering. The fierce Comanches were as yet untamed, and the cruel, vicious "Tawakhannies" and "Karankuhuas" roamed the coast and the mouths of rivers inflicting all manner of depredations upon the settlers.[54]

Another very serious problem was the apathetic view toward education by many Texans. "Love of education has never been characteristic of early settlers of America."[55] Most frontiersmen were highly suspicious of and antagonistic toward anyone who demonstrated any amount of education beyond the barest rudiments. Even though the majority of the Baptists in Texas would follow their able leaders, they were few in number and widely scattered—there were only about 1,400 Baptists scattered throughout Texas in small villages or farms miles apart.[56] The founders of Baylor University must have realized that the burden of maintaining the school would therefore fall

---

[50]**Ibid.,** p. 402.

[51]Rev. Olin W. Nail (ed.), **Texas Methodist Centennial Yearbook** (Elgin, Texas, 1934), pp. 45-49.

[52]Eby, **Education in Texas,** p. 99.

[53]Lane, **History of Education,** p. 65.

[54]Carl, Prince of Solms-Braunfels, **Texas 1844-1845** (Houston: the Anson Jones Press, 1936), p. 41.

[55]Link, **Historical and Biographical Magazine,** p. 468.

[56]**Supra,** p. 6.

upon the small number of Baptist leaders who were farsighted enough to see the needs of the people of Texas.

There were two major reasons in the minds of these pioneers for establishment of a Baptist university. The founders first of all realized that the sound learning provided for by such a university would greatly increase "moral power" and thereby increase the future prosperity and influence of the Baptist denomination in Texas.[57] Probably the strongest motive for establishing the school was the desire to prepare an educated ministry so necessary in bringing respectability to the denomination. With the influx of "enterprising and intelligent citizens" from the other states, there was the need for a well-educated ministry to mold, harmonize, and direct the churches. The proposed university would provide ministers with the education they needed.[58]

In 1849 the *South-Western Baptist Chronicle,* a widely read denominational paper, printed a letter from Rev. R. H. Taliaferro. In this letter Taliaferro gave the aims of the university. He first mentioned that the prime reason was to furnish Texas with an educated ministry, then he suggested that the school would also "elevate the standing of our denomination." He felt that Baptists throughout the South must have literary institutions or "suffer the neglect, and even the contempt, of this intellectual age." Other denominations were establishing schools; the Baptists should do likewise. A Baptist school in Texas would eliminate the necessity of Baptists having to send their children to the colleges of other denominations or out of the state. Most important of all, a Baptist university would provide an "attitude of religious fervor," aid in the salvation of its students, and would unite the ministers through the comradeship obtained by attending school together. Taliaferro also felt that Baylor University could best prepare ministers for the particular ways of Texas, and that missionaries to Mexico could be better prepared in Texas.[59]

There is considerable doubt concerning the events preceding the granting of the school's charter. The authorship of the charter is traditionally ascribed to Tryon. According to this

---

[57]Baptist State Convention of Texas, **Organization Proceedings** (Anderson County, Texas, 1848), p. 10.

[58]Baptist State Convention of Texas, **Fifth Annual Session** (Marshall, Texas, 1852), p. 10.

[59]**South-Western Baptist Chronicle** (New Orleans, Louisiana), November 17, 1849.

tradition, he wrote the charter in its entirety and then submitted the finished product to Judge Baylor who approved it as originally drafted.[60] There is, however, a possibility that Judge Baylor dictated the charter while Tryon wrote it.[61] In either case, Tryon seems to have done the actual writing.

There is also some uncertainty as to just how Baylor University received its name. Several names were considered. Judge Baylor's petition for the charter of a university was presented to the Senate of the Republic of Texas on December 28, 1844. The petition was not considered until January 3, 1845 at which time Senator John A. Greer, for the State of the Republic Committee, recommended the incorporation of "San Jacinto University." The Senate again considered the petition on January 7. At that time Senator George A. Patillo changed the name from "San Jacinto" to "Milam University." The next day Patillo moved to strike out "Milam" and insert "Baylor," and the bill was passed by the Senate and sent to the House.[62]

Evidently the question of a name for the proposed school did not arise until the charter was being considered by the Senate. There are three versions of just what happened at this point. According to one version when the question was brought to Judge Baylor and Rev. Tryon, Baylor suggested "Tryon." Tryon protested, saying that he feared people would think he supported the idea of a school for his own honor. Tryon then wrote "Baylor" in the proper space. Baylor then objected, saying that he did not feel worthy of it, and since he had given the largest contribution for the school, people would feel that he had done so for his own glory. However, Tryon and Vice-President Kenneth L. Anderson would have it no other way; so the charter went again before the Senate with "Baylor" as the name of the university.[63]

Another version suggests that when Tryon proposed "Baylor" as the name of the university, Baylor objected on the grounds that his activity in politics had incurred political prejudices which might seriously retard the school. Tryon insisted, but the friendly dispute was not settled until other members of the Education Society were called in. These members sided

---

[60]Harry Haynes, **The Life and Writings of Dr. Rufus C. Burleson** (published by Mrs. Georgia Jenkins Burleson, 1901), p. 103.

[61]Carroll, **Texas Baptists,** p. 230.

[62]Letter from Herbert Gambrell to Guy B. Harrison, Jr., July 25, 1947 (Baylor at Independence Papers, Texas Collection, Baylor University).

[63]Carroll, **Texas Baptists,** p. 229.

with Tryon and insisted that "Baylor University" be inserted in the space provided for the name.[64] A less complimentary version states that when Tryon suggested the name "Baylor" out of modesty and courtesy, Baylor was "sufficiently lacking in delicacy" and accepted the suggestion without much ado.[65]

After the matter of the name was somehow settled, and the Senate passed the recommendation on to the House, the charter was finally passed on January 29, 1845. President Anson Jones signed the bill into law on February 1. The charter named as members of the Board of Trustees R. E. B. Baylor, I. G. Thomas, Albert C. Horton, Edward Taylor, James S. Lester, R. B. Jarmin, James Huckins, Nelson Kavanaugh, O. Drake, Eli Mercer, Aaron Shannon, James Farquhar, Albert Haynes, Robert S. Armstead, and William M. Tryon.[66] The Board was given the power to receive any gifts for the institution not to exceed $100,000; was authorized to transact all necessary business; could appoint a president and professors and prescribe the curriculum, and could fix salaries and expel any student.[67] Thus, with the granting of a charter by the Republic of Texas, what had been only an idea had become a legal reality.

---

[64] Haynes, **Life and Writings of Burleson,** pp. 103-104.

[65] Herbert Gambrell, "The Early Baylor University 1841-1861" (unpublished Masters Thesis, Department of History, Southern Methodist University, 1924), p. 16.

[66] Photostat of the original act (Texas Collection, Baylor University).

[67] **Laws of the Republic of Texas 5th Congress** (Houston, 1841), pp. 84-87.

2

Baylor University 1845-1851

IT WAS one thing to secure a legal charter for a university and quite another thing to actually get one established and functioning. The first item of business was to get the Board of Trustees together so that plans could be made and action taken. Even this simple task proved to be not so simple—the first attempt at a meeting was made on April 7, 1845. Not enough trustees showed up to constitute a quorum, so the members present postponed the meeting until May 15.[1] On that date the Board again met, not at Independence as on the first try, but at Brenham—this time a quorum was present. Those attending were R. E. B. Baylor, I. G. Thomas, James L. Lester, R. B. Jarman, N. Kavanaugh, Oran Drake, James L. Farquhar, A. G. Haynes, E. W. Taylor, and Hosea Garrett as proxy for Tryon. The first order of business was the election of Baylor as President of the Board. A committee was then set up to formulate the rules for procedure that the Board would follow in its deliberations. Kavanaugh then proposed that the trustees choose the location of the university, but the others felt that more time was needed in order to ascertain all of the possibilities. This decision was therefore postponed until the next meeting.[2] More than likely there had been much interest generated by the possibility of the new school being located in one of the communities around Brenham. Most communities were very anxious to have such establishments in their town because of the prestige and added income. The Trustees wisely postponed the decision so that more communities could offer their proposals, and the Trustees would have the comfortable advantage of being asked instead of asking.

On the morning of October 13, 1845 the Board met to con-

[1]Minutes, April 7, 1845, p. 7.

[2]Minutes, May 15 and 16, 1845, pp. 7-8.

sider proposals for the location of the school. Four towns submitted proposals—Eli Mercer presented the proposition from Travis in Austin County; Aaron Shannon for Shannon Prairie; E. W. Taylor for Independence; and a "Rev. Mr. Stovall" for Huntsville. After hearing the proposals the Board appointed a committee to examine the offers, and then the meeting was adjourned for the morning.[3]

The Board reassembled at two o'clock that afternoon and received the committee's report. Valuing all uncultivated land, except the town lots, at seventy-five cents an acre, and fixing the price of town lots at the price they could be sold for cash, the committee reported the following valuations: Travis $3,586.25; Huntsville $5,417.09; Independence $7,925.00; Shannon Prairie $4,725.09. The Board then voted by secret ballot; Independence received ten votes, and Huntsville one vote.[4]

E. W. Taylor, who presented the proposal for Independence was a trustee even though he was not a Baptist. He was an enterprising merchant of Independence and was naturally anxious to have the institution in his locality. To assure the trustees' decision in his favor, he added a lot with a two-story building to his original bid just before the balloting.[5] Taylor had acquired this property in a round-about way. This building and lot, known as Academy Hill, was first owned by Mrs. Ann Koontz. In 1838 she had transferred the four acres to the trustees of Independence Academy for $40.[6] In 1841 a suit was filed against the trustees of the academy, and the school's property was taken for debts incurred. At a sheriff's sale in 1845 the land and the building were sold to Edward M. Taylor, representing the firm of Root & Taylor, for $350.[7] This two-story building would be the only one used by Baylor University for the first five years of her existence.

In view of the situation in 1845, Independence was an excellent site for a university. Besides having offered the highest bid, there were other good reasons why the town was a good location. Independence was in Washington County, which at that time led the state in wealth, population, and influence. The town was the center of a settlement of prosperous, intelligent,

---

[3]Minutes, October 13, 1845, p. 9.
[4]Ibid., p. 10.
[5]Ray, Austin Colony, pp. 38, 40.
[6]Copy of the original deed (Baylor at Independence Papers, Texas Collection, Baylor University).
[7]Copy of the original deed (Baylor at Independence Papers, Texas Collection, Baylor University).

and refined people. Many of the university's active supporters lived in or near the town.[8] Independence was important historically; Baylor was to be located not far from Washington-on-the-Brazos, where the Texas Declaration of Independence was written.[9] Independence had already gained a reputation as the "Athens of Texas" by having a girls' boarding school established there in 1835, and the Independence Academy in 1837.[10]

In December 1845, the Board met in Independence to select the best site in town for the school. The Public Square, the plot of ground donated by W. W. Allen,[11] and the Academy Hill were the sites suggested. Allen Hill received seven votes; Academy Hill received one vote.

One reason why the trustees chose Allen Hill was the location of a quarry of fine stone near the hill. The building committee had decided that stone structures would be the cheapest and most durable type of construction.[12]

With the site chosen and all preliminary business taken care of, the trustees wasted no time in beginning actual operation of the school. They decided to repair the two-story building donated by Taylor and to begin a preparatory school as soon as possible. Acting upon a motion by Farquhar the Board elected Henry F. Gillette teacher of the preparatory school. Baylor, Tryon, and Taylor were appointed to meet with Mr. Gillette and make the necessary arrangements. They were to offer him an annual salary of not more than $800.[13] Most universities of that day had as a part of the institution a preparatory department to provide whatever the students needed for admittance into the university department. Usually the preparatory department contained the bulk of the institution's enrollment as the university department was very selective and quite difficult.

Henry F. Gillette was an enthusiastic supporter of education. He was well known by several of the trustees. Earlier in 1845 he along with Judge Baylor had signed a newspaper notice stating the educational needs of Texas.[14] He was well acquaint-

[8]Link, **Historical and Biographical Magazine**, p. 469.

[9]Lane, **Education in Texas**, p. 65.

[10]Charles F. Schmidt, **History of Washington County** (San Antonio: Naylor Company, 1947), p. 61.

[11]For the token price of one dollar, Mr. and Mrs. Allen gave some land (6.3 acres) known as Wind Mill or Allen Hill (photostat of the original deed in the Texas Collection, Baylor University).

[12]Minutes, December 7, 1845, pp. 11-12.

[13]Minutes, January 12, 1846, pp. 13-15.

[14]**Telegraph and Texas Register** (Houston), November 19, 1845.

ed with Tryon since Tryon had performed the ceremony at Gillette's marriage in 1842.[15] In 1838 at the age of twenty-three, Gillette came to Texas and taught at Washington-on-the-Brazos until 1841. In 1841 he began teaching at the Independence Academy until it closed that same year.[16] Gillette's character, his background as an educator, and his friendship with Baylor and Tryon provided good reasons for his selection by the trustees.

The preparatory department opened on the morning of May 18, 1846 after a few days delay until the building was ready for occupancy. Classes were held on the first floor of the frame building on Academy Hill. The building had needed extensive repairs; the inside walls needed boards, and workmen had to install fourteen desks and a stage before the school could begin its exercises. The upper room could not be used because there was no floor between the two levels.

Except for the slight delay, the school had a good beginning. The preparatory school offered a variety of courses so as to attract the largest enrollment possible. Reading, writing, and spelling cost the student $8.00 a term. For $10.00 more the student could receive instruction in geography, arithmetic, and grammar. Higher level of instruction included philosophy, rhetoric, chemistry, and higher branches of mathematics could be obtained for $23.00 a term. Latin and Greek, mandatory for college entrance, were also offered at $15.00 each per term. The school received no student for less than half a term, and students were charged tuition in proportion to the length of their stay. Private families provided board, including lodging and washing for $8.00 a month.

Although the school opened on May 18, 1846, the regular school year did not begin until the first Monday in June. The regular school year consisted of two terms of five months each. The first term ran from June through October, 1846 with the month of November for vacation. The second term was from December 1, 1846 through April, 1847, with a vacation through the month of May.[17] The first year opened with twenty-four students, increasing to seventy before the end of the first term.

---

[15]August A. Grusendorf, "The Baptists and Education in Washington County, 1845-1875" (unpublished theme, Texas Collection, Baylor University).

[16]Mrs. W. A. Wood, "Prof. Henry F. Gillette Lives in His Deeds," **Gulf Coast Baptist,** September 18, 1941.

[17]Minutes, May 19, 1846, pp. 19-21.

The tuition due amounted to $468.06, of which the school had collected $347.00 by the end of the term. The second term began with fifty-one students, and the enrollment increased to around seventy by the end of the school year. Sickness and "other obstacles" did much to interfere with the success of the second term. By the end of the second term the school had received only $78.00 of the $512.39 due from tuition.[18]

Gillette seems to have done all of the teaching during most of the first year. The Board appointed a committee to find an assistant, but no report indicated that they were successful. Gillette, however, seemed pleased with his work the first year. In a letter to Ashbel Smith he stated "I now feel my self settled at the town of Independence, have made arrangements to buy a few acres of land for (*sic*) to work, and shall soon commence building me a house. I have a pleasant though laborious school. I now have 51 scholars, and it is constantly increasing. If they will make my salary $1,000 a year I will stay a long time with them."[19]

On Sundays the various denominations held services in the school building. The Baptists used the building on the first Sunday of each month and the Methodists on the next Sunday. Any "Christian denomination" that desired could use the building on the third Sunday of the month. The Presbyterians met on the last Sunday of each month.[20] This religious toleration demonstrated by the trustees has persisted throughout Baylor's history.

While the preparatory department was progressing nicely, the trustees made plans to get the university department started. On January 12, 1846, Rev. Henry Lee Graves of Georgia was elected president of the university on a motion from Judge Baylor, and the secretary, E. W. Taylor, was instructed to notify him by letter.[21]

Independence Jany 20 1846

Rev. Henry L. Graves

Dear Sir:

I have the honor of informing you that at a meeting of the Board of Trustees of the Baylor Univer-

---

[18]Minutes, April 27, 1847, p. 27.

[19]Copy of a letter from Henry F. Gillette to Ashbel Smith, August 15, 1846 (Texas Collection, Baylor University).

[20]Minutes, October 8, 1846, pp. 23-24.

[21]Minutes, January 12, 1846, p. 14.

sity convened at this place on the 12 Inst. you were unanimously elected President of the Institution.

I would be extremely gratified in hearing from you.

Respectfully
Yr ob'dt Svt
E. W. Taylor[22]

When the Board met in May, Graves' letter of acceptance was read, and a second letter was sent to him in acknowledgment of his letter and informing of his appointment as Agent for the State of Georgia to collect subscriptions for the institution.[23] The trustees did not overlook any chance of getting money for the struggling school.

Graves was a well-educated man, being a graduate of the University of North Carolina and Hamilton Theological Seminary.[24] He was a dignified "princely gentleman," a good scholar, and a "splendid school man."[25] He therefore seemed a good choice for the presidency of the new university.

On February 4, 1847, Graves appeared before the Board, and immediately entered upon his duties as president.[26] Since the regular collegiate year did not begin until June, Graves spent the first four months either getting things ready for the oncoming work or teaching in the preparatory school or both.

The first collegiate year of the university consisted of two terms, the first was five months in length, and the second, six months. The first term began on June 1, 1847, and ended on December 1, 1847 with the month of December comprising the first vacation. The second term was from January 1 to June 1, 1848. The entire month of June was a vacation period. The tuition was set at $25.00 payable in advance.[27]

The activities of the Collegiate Department during the first year are somewhat obscure, but it is doubtful that the department had many pupils. Although the preparatory department was a year old, there was no mention of any student being ready for college courses. Both departments held classes in the Academy Building, and both the male and females used

---

[22]Letter from E. W. Taylor to Henry L. Graves, January 20, 1846, quoted in Gambrell, "Early Baylor," appendix, p. iv½.

[23]**Ibid.**

[24]Letter from R. C. Burleson to Richard Burleson, February 6, 1854 (Burleson Papers, Texas Collection, Baylor University).

[25]Carroll, **Texas Baptists,** p. 233.

[26]Minutes, February 4, 1847, p. 25.

[27]Minutes, April 27, 1847, p. 28.

the same building, but probably at different times. In January, 1848, Graves reported that there were about one hundred students in both departments during the first term. Prospects were bright, but more "laborers in the field" were needed.[28]

The early years of the institution were anything but easy ones for the trustees. The Board of Trustees was beset with problems from 1848 to 1851, the chief one being the lack of sufficient finances. With the expiration of his contract in 1848, Gillette tendered his resignation, stating that after eight years of teaching the youth of Texas he felt it best to retire and "let others endure the hardships that I have endured."[29] The inability of the school to pay a regular salary was a more realistic reason for his resignation. Upon the exit of Gillette, President Graves took over the Preparatory Department. He selected the teachers, paid them at his own expense, and received all tuition of the department.[30] Although plagued with problems, the trustees remained optimistic. Shortly after Gillette's resignation, they decided to construct the first permanent building on Allen Hill.[31] The trustees thus ended their deliberations for 1848 with the hope of future prosperity.

In some ways, the year 1849 was considerably brighter. James Huckins, the university's agent, came before the Board and presented his first report, which was favorable and encouraging. As further encouragement, Judge A. S. Lipscomb, recently appointed to the Board of Trustees, met with the Board and offered to give lectures on law at the university. The Board quickly established a professorship of law. The duties of the professorship were discharged *gratis* by Judges Lipscomb and Baylor and others. The trustees were also able to provide for much needed and extensive repairs on the Academy Building.[32]

The first problem of discipline arose in 1849. The Board approved President Graves' suspension of Orlando Harris. Since the school needed students, the Board felt inclined to be lenient —they suggested that if Harris presented a "proper degree of regret" for his actions and satisfied President Graves as to his future conduct, he should be restored to his previous standing.

[28]**South-Western Baptist Chronicle** (New Orleans, Louisiana), January 8, 1848.

[29]Copy of a letter from Henry Gillette to Ashbel Smith, August 15, 1848 (Texas Collection, Baylor University).

[30]Minutes, June 1 and 2, 1848, pp. 32-33.

[31]Minutes, June 3, 1848, p. 35.

[32]Minutes, April 2 and 4, 1849, pp. 40-41.

There was no mention of just what Harris did to cause his suspension, but it seems not have have been too serious. Since there was no further mention of the affair, the student probably was allowed to resume his school work.[33]

An even more unpleasant task came before the trustees as a result concerning a fellow trustee. The Board received certain reports unfavorable to the moral character of Oran Drake (it seems that he was seen on several occasions entering an establishment that served strong drink). The Board of Trustees requested his resignation.[34]

Conditions continued to worsen—in 1850 the trustees earnestly tried to solve the ever-pressing financial difficulties, but they were not successful. This constant, unsolved problem was very discouraging to Graves. On June 14, 1851, he tendered his resignation. Graves had struggled under many handicaps and had made very little apparent progress. Graves felt that the school could not continue to operate much longer.[35] Graves was also in bad health; his throat had been giving him trouble for some years, and for more than a year before his resignation he could not speak above a whisper.[36] After trying to persuade Graves to remain with the school, and having no success, the Board appointed A. S. Lipscomb, J. W. D. Creath, A. G. Haynes, R. E. B. Baylor, nad T. J. Jackson as a committee to secure a new president.[37]

Throughout the first five years, financing the operation of the university was the major problem faced by the Board of Trustees. Money received from tuition was not sufficient to pay the salaries, much less the other things needed. Early in 1847 the trustees appointed R. C. Burleson, who had juts arrived in Texas, agent for the university. He traveled through Kentucky, Ohio, Mississippi, and Alabama collecting what he could. Burleson was able to acquire some needed apparatus and books but not much money.[38] Later in 1847 Rev. James Huckins was appointed agent for the school. The Board offered to pay him $1,000 a year (which they did not have) plus expenses.[39] Huckins agreed to be agent on certain conditions. He asked that the Board make no further appropriations until all the liabilities of

[33]Minutes, June 14, 1849, p. 42.
[34]Minutes, August 21, 1849, p. 42.
[35]Dawson, **A Century with Texas Baptists**, p. 10.
[36]Gambrell, "Early Baylor," p. 49.
[37]Minutes, June 16, 1851, p. 52.
[38]Haynes, "R. C. Burleson," p. 53.
[39]Minutes, December 22, 1847, p. 30.

the school were liquidated, and to insure him that finances would be handled properly because the donors would be looking to him in some degree for the "judicious expenditure of their money."[40] Huckins acted as agent for five years, traveling over most of Texas and the South. From Texans he received wild lands, beeves, cows, calves, dried hides, and mustangs, but very little money. In Southern states he secured $1,300 cash, some books, and other apparatus. In five years he obtained some $30,000 in promissory notes for endowments.[41] Without these funds Baylor University could not have continued operations. In the spring of 1849 Huckins made his first report to the Board of Trustees. He had collected $9,345.62 in subscriptions, $3,338 in stock and labor, and $811.12 in cash. Of the money promised by subscriptions, $2,061.50 was promised by April 1, 1849, and $1,775.50 by April 1, 1850.[42]

Even with the money brought in by Huckins' efforts, there was never enough. In 1848, just prior to Gillette's resignation, the treasurer reported that the school owed President Graves $1,200 and Gillette $800 for their services. Ten members of the Board each agreed to pay each of the men $20. Eli Mercer promised to pay the remainder of the salary if it did not exceed $150. The tutors were to also be paid only in part from the tuition collected.[43]

In 1850 the treasurer reported that $730 cash had been collected. Of that amount $580 was already appropriated, leaving only $150, not much on which to run a school.[44] The Board appointed a committee to prepare a circular letter setting forth the needs of the institution and pleading for contributions. The Board also ruled that all students entering the school would have to pay a fee of $1.00 for the maintenance of the building. A committee also proposed the selling of scholarships as a means of raising $10,000 for the endowment of the presidency. A permanent scholarship would cost $500. It would entitle the holder of the certificate to receive instruction in any classes he desired. The scholarship would take the name of the first purchaser. A family scholarship would cost $100 each if five or more were purchased. This scholarship entitled the holder to instruction in any classes he desired for his sons, daughters,

---

[40]Gambrell, "Early Baylor," appendix.
[41]Link, **Historical and Biographical Magazine**, p. 186.
[42]Minutes, April 2, 1849, p. 37.
[43]Minutes, June 1 and 2, 1848, pp. 32-33.
[44]Minutes, June 13, 1850, pp. 45-46.

step-children, or orphans under guardianship. A church scholarship would cost $200. It would entitle any church or association to send one young man for any instruction desired. Individual scholarships cost $150 and entitled the individual named in the certificate to any instruction desired. There was also a charity scholarship costing $50; it entitled any person named in the certificate to any instruction desired, providing he was in "indigent circumstances." These scholarships would exempt the students from payment of tuition only, and were solely for the Collegiate Department. The Board appointed Graves, J. W. D. Creath, B. H. Stribling, R. C. Burleson, George Baines and R. H. Taliaferro as agents to sell the scholarships.[45]

The trustees did not overlook any possibility for obtaining badly needed financial support. Since its organization in 1848, the Baptist State Convention had given no real support to the struggling institution. In 1850 the state legislature granted, upon request from the trustees, an amendment to the university's charter giving the convention the power to select the trustees. The trustees hoped that giving the convention some responsibility would also encourage other tangible response like definite financial assistance. This strategy did not appear to work. However in 1851 prospects improved. The convention was invited to hold its annual meeting in the newly completed college building on Allen Hill. On the evening of June 16, 1851 Judge Lipscomb addressed the convention, giving reasons why a permanent endowment for the presidency of Baylor was necessary. The plan of the trustees was then read to the group. The Board proposed to raise $10,000 through gifts and subscriptions. Sums of $10 or less were to be paid immediately. Sums between $10 and $50 were to be paid in one, two, or three-year installments with 8% per annum interest. Sums of $50 or more could be paid outright or retained until called for at the option of the subscriber. Lipscomb, Eli Mercer and Jesse Witt made a final plea before the convention which resulted in $5,335 being subscribed immediately.[46]

On the last day of the convention the Education Committee presented its report containing four resolutions. The report stressed the need of an educated ministry and urged churches to seek out promising young men and help them financially to

---

[45]Minutes, June 15, 1850, pp. 47-48.

[46]Minutes of the Fifth Annual Session of the Baptist State Convention of Texas, 1851 (Washington, Texas: Texas Ranger Office, 1851), p. 7.

prepare for the ministry. Pastors should present the need of an educated ministry to their congregations at least once a year, and adopt some plan whereby regular contributions could be made to the cause of ministerial education. The Board of Trustees of Baylor was urged to obtain an agent to secure the endowment of the presidency. All of the members of the convention were admonished to pledge cooperation with the Board through prayers, sympathies and money (especially money), in securing the needed endowment.[47] With the apparent support of the Baptist State Convention, the trustees were greatly encouraged, and with renewed vigor they went about the task of finding a new president and putting the school on a secure financial and academic foundation.

---

[47]Ibid., p. 13.

3

The Burleson Administration

ON JUNE 17, 1851, the Board of Trustees unanimously elected Rufus Columbus Burleson to the presidency of Baylor University. On June 18, Burleson came before the Board and formally accepted the position.[1] Burleson immediately insisted that the males and females be separated in all school work; a male and a female department were therefore designated, and Horace Clark was appointed as principal of the female division. Burleson with the male department would move into the newly constructed college building, while the female department would remain in the Old Academy Building.[2] Clark was present at the June 18 meeting, and he accepted the appointment on the condition that he be entitled to the tuition derived from his department.[3]

Through the able leadership of Burleson and Clark, Baylor University was to enjoy almost a decade of prosperity. In 1851 Baylor was one of two colleges in the entire state,[4] and from 1851 to the Civil War, Baylor was one of the few institutions offering genuine college work and graduating students with degrees.[5]

Both Burleson and Clark were honest, hard-working, strong-willed men dedicated to the success of their particular departments. Their efforts brought prosperity and prestige to the university, but they also precipitated a crisis which not only threatened to push the school into oblivion, but caused a schism within the Baptist denomination in Texas.

Rufus Burleson was a strong, forceful man dedicated to education and proud of his accomplishments. He demanded ex-

[1]Minutes, June 17-18, 1851, p. 54.
[2]Carroll, **Texas Baptists,** p. 234.
[3]Minutes, June 18, 1851, p. 54.
[4]Eby, **Education in Texas,** p. 154.
[5]**Ibid.,** p. 135.

cellence in all endeavors from his students as well as for himself. In a letter to his brother, Richard, Burleson demonstrated this zeal toward excellence:

> I also devote much time to Rhetorical exercises. An orator can shake the world. And why are we not orators? We can be if we will strive as Demosthenes did. If I am not an orator in ten years then do not call me Brother.[6]

In spite of, or because of his stern, uncompromising spirit, the male students respected, admired and perhaps even loved him. One student's reaction to his first meeting with Burleson was recorded in a Baptist paper of the 1850's:

> And while already we were shrinking back from the piercing glance, the hand of cordial welcome was extended. He is courteous and polite, yet we stand in awe! We do not dread him, for we love him.[7]

Burleson was a stern disciplinarian; he saw nothing incongruous in first praying with a young man and then taking him out and administering a sound flogging.[8]

Clark, although as strong-willed as Burleson, seemed to have had less of a stern nature than did his fellow educator. One visitor to Baylor considered Clark one of the most affable men that he had ever met, and his wife even surpassed him in graciousness and politeness.[9] Judge Baylor thought very highly of Clark, and in his memoirs the judge gave a good description of him:

> Bro. Clark was of medium height with a figure not denoting great sinual or muscular strength; blue eyes, light hair and complection (*sic*), features regular and well formed of the Grecian mold; the base of his forhead (*sic*) strongly marked and projecting which showed at once he was no ordinary man; with manners uniformly kind and polite.[10]

With the college off to a fresh new start, the Board of Trustees met several times in June and August of 1851 in order to conduct all of the pressing business. The Board decided to

---

[6]Letter from R. C. Burleson, Sept. 26, 1847 (R. C. Burleson Papers, Texas Collection, Baylor University).

[7]**Texas Baptist Herald** (Houston), March 18, 1857.

[8]Eby, **Education in Texas,** pp. 139-140.

[9]**Texas Baptist** (Anderson, Texas), Sept. 9, 1858.

[10]R. E. B. Baylor Manuscript.

commence school on the first Monday in August. The building committee was asked to have repairs made upon the Old Academy Building, now called the Female Academy, and to purchase a house for Clark and his family.[11] Since a title for the Female Academy had still not been procured from Root & Taylor, A. G. Haynes was authorized to get it as soon as possible.[12]

To take care of the expected increase in enrollment, two teachers were appointed by the Board, and a committee of three was asked to meet with Burleson and Clark to make out regular courses of study for each classification of the male and female students in the collegiate and preparatory departments. The trustees also felt it necessary to either build or buy a dormitory or boarding house for the male students in the near future.[13]

Tuition for the collegiate department was set at $25. In the preparatory department the tuition varied. Elementary English classes cost $10 whereas a course of study including English grammar, geography, arithmetic, and composition amounted to $13. Foreign languages each cost $10, and course of study encompassing ancient languages, mathematics, natural sciences, and moral and intellectual philosophy cost $15. Music lessons cost $25 for either pianoforte or guitar, but vocal music lessons were free of charge. For $10 a month, room and board, including washing was provided.[14]

According to the first catalogue published by the university, the 1851-1852 school year began on the first Monday in August, 1851, and ended June 1, 1852. A total of 165 students attended the institution under Burleson's and Clark's first year of leadership. The male department gave instruction to 94 students, 77 of which were in the preparatory department, with 6 sophomores and 11 freshmen in the collegiate department.[15] The female department had a total of 71 students during the school year, 53 of which were in the preparatory school. The collegiate department was composed of 2 juniors, 7 sophomores and 7 freshmen.[16]

Each student in the collegiate departments had four classes

[11]Minutes, June 18, 1851, p. 55.
[12]Minutes, Aug. 2, 1851, p. 56.
[13]**Ibid.**, pp. 56-57.
[14]**Catalogue of the Trustees, Officers, and Students of Baylor University; Independence, Washington County, Texas, 1851-1852.** Hereafter cited as Catalogue, p. 13.
[15]**Ibid.**, pp. 3-5.
[16]**Ibid.**, p. 11.

a day, while the preparatory students had even more. Compositions and declamations were required of all students semimonthly.[17]

The preparatory course of study lasted two years, but if after that time the student was still not advanced enough to enter the collegiate department, further instruction was given. Students could enter the preparatory school at any stage of advancement.

Students were admitted to the collegiate department only after they had passed an examination encompassing Caesar, Virgil, Cicero's Selected Orations, algebra, and the Latin and Greek grammar. In order to advance to a higher class the college student had to pass an examination over all of the subjects previously taken.[18]

The instructors kept a daily record of the attendance, conduct, and recitations of each student. Also a weekly summary of each student was recorded in a permanent file so that the student's standing could be determined at any time. The students were required to attend prayers in the College Chapel every morning and evening. Although church attendance was strongly encouraged by the school officials, no one was forced to attend. Those students who chose to attend church services could attend the church of their choice.[19]

Once the school's program was under way, the trustees began to consider ways to improve the institution. They inquired into the possibility of organizing a theological department in connection with the other collegiate work, but were informed by Burleson that such a department was not possible at that time. However, as there were some ministerial students in the school, some arrangements were deemed necessary. The board recommended that these young men be placed in a theological class, and that Burleson give them what instruction he could. Baines was also requested to deliver some lectures on Pastoral Theology to the class.[20]

In the latter part of 1851 the trustees began a concerted effort to increase the financial stability of the school. The Board sent a request through the *Southwest Baptist,* the *Christian Index,* and the *New York Recorder* for Huckins to return to Independence as soon as possible so that the trustees could re-

---

[17]Ibid., p. 7.
[18]Ibid,. p. 8.
[19]Ibid., pp. 7-8.
[20]Minutes, Dec. 13, 1851, p. 61.

ceive his report and make plans accordingly.[21] Since the endowment fund for the presidency was nearing $10,000, the trustees decided to increase it. Burleson and Creath each volunteered to raise $2,000, and Hosea Garrett promised to raise $500.[22] When Burleson informed the Board that he planned to travel to different parts of the state during the December holidays, he was authorized to collect promised subscriptions and accept new ones.[23]

In January, 1852, Huckins came before the Board and presented both a written and a verbal report. He had collected $1,300 in cash which the Board applied to Burleson's salary with the condition that one poor young ministerial student be educated free of charge for every $600 of the above sum. J. W. D. Creath also reported that he had collected a little cash and $300 in subscriptions. Gratitude was extended to the two men for their efforts, and Huckins was again elected agent for the university.[24]

With the comfortable experience of having some money in the treasury, the trustees began to pay the schools debts. Creath received $13.56 for his service as a collecting agent. James L. Smith and D. B. Madden were each paid $15 for some merchandise the school had purchased earlier. W. H. Cleveland received $250 as partial payment of a note he held on the trustees.[25] Later in the year Cleveland was paid the balance of the note.[26] The treasurer was authorized to pay a local merchant, F. W. Robertson, $200 plus a load of sugar and molasses for payment of merchandise that had been purchased for the college on credit.[27] Nelson Kavanaugh, one of the trustees, finally received full payment for some window blinds he had provided for the new college building on Allen Hill.[28] These various payments were the first of any large amount mentioned in the minutes, and they indicated that the university's finances were indeed improving. Another indication of the improved financial condition of the school was the purchase of a house costing $1,200. Horace Clark, the principal of the female department,

---

[21]**Ibid.,** p. 60
[22]**Ibid.,** p. 61.
[23]Minutes, Nov. 4, 1851, p. 59.
[24]Minutes, Jan. 22, 1852, pp. 63-64.
[25]**Ibid.,** p. 64.
[26]Minutes, June 10, 1852, p. 66.
[27]Minutes, Jan. 22, 1852, p. 64.
[28]**Minutes,** June 10, 1852, p. 66.
[29]Minutes, June 11, 1852, p. 68.

was to have the house and premises for $100 a year rent which he could discharge in improvements.

Toward the end of the 1851-52 school year, the greatly encouraged trustees set forth the goals for the coming year, the primary goal being the payment of all debts by collecting all subscriptions due. The trustees further hoped to establish clear title to all properties given to the institution, establish a fund for the endowment of the professorships of the male department, erect dormitories and a boarding house for the male students, and repair the Female Academy.[30]

The fall term for the school year 1852-53 began on July 20, and continued for five months to the Christmas holidays.[31] Beginning in 1853 the school year was changed to consist of only one term of ten months beginning on the first Monday of March and with vacations in January and February. This change was made due to the requests of many of the parents, and at the advice of the school's teachers. From July, 1852, to December, 1853, the male department reached an enrollment of 93, with 16 in the collegiate department and 77 in the preparatory school.[32] The female department had an enrollment of about 69 students, giving a total of about 162 for both departments.[33]

On January 2, 1853 an event took place which greatly increased Burleson's prestige and happiness—his marriage to Miss Georgia Jenkins, the daughter of a prominent family in Texas.[34]

Burleson worked earnestly at his task moulding the school into an institution that Texas Baptists could speak of with pride. Although Burleson wrote to his brother, Richard, "No human knows what toil and labor I have expended on this university," he was quite pleased with his position as he also wrote "My present situation is easy and lucrative. My income is about $1,000 per annum. We have a glorious school here."[35] At the Texas Baptist Convention in 1852 the education committee reported that Baylor University had prospered beyond "most sanguine expectations." A new college building had been erected (the stone building on Allen Hill); the number of students

---

[30]Minutes, June 10, 1852, p. 67.
[31]Catalogue, 1851-52, p. 13.
[32]Catalogue, 1852-53, p. 7.
[33]Letter from R. C. Burleson to Richard Burleson, November 8, 1852 (R. C. Burleson Papers, Texas Collection, Baylor University).
[34]Marriage certificate (R. C. Burleson Papers, Texas Collection, Baylor University).
[35]Letter from R. C. Burleson to Richard Burleson, Nov. 8, 1852 (R. C. Burleson Papers, Texas Collection, Baylor University).

had increased, and the best news of all was that the treasury was in a "healthy condition." The committee further reported that the endowment of the presidency was nearly $10,000; the school employed six instructors and was supplied with good chemical and philosophical apparatus including a small but valuable library.[36] So pleased with the success of the university were the Baptist leaders that when a motion was brought before the convention concerning establishing a female institute near Tyler, the convention stated that it did not feel it in its design to aid any institution other than Baylor University.[37]

With the appearance of some success and prosperity, the trustees labored faithfully to maintain Baylor's success. The trustees felt it necessary to first pay the salaries of the president and then of the other instructors before any other financial obligations were considered.[38] Hosea Garrett, president of the Board, recorded a large number of subscriptions in 1852, including $200 from Judge Baylor,[39] and about 280 acres were donated to the school by various people.[40] The trustees did not let this success cloud the picture—they were not going to sit back and rest upon their laurels. The trustees felt that constant improvement was necessary due to the increasing demands being placed upon the school by the constantly increasing number of pupils, the rapid increase of the state's population, and the constantly increasing demands of the denomination and of the people at large upon the institution.[41] To increase the efficiency of the school the trustees decided to adopt a code of laws.[42]

In July, 1853 James Huckins made his final report as agent of the university. For his services Huckins received $803, $215 of which was paid with available funds; $437 was paid by a draft on R. E. B. Baylor, and a note payable on January 1, 1854 was given by the trustees for the remaining $151.[43]

The school year of 1854 began on March 1 and continued without vacation until the close of the winter examinations which began the third winter in December. The one vacation

---

[36]**The Fifth Annual Session of the Baptist State Convention of Texas, Marshall, Texas, 1852** (Lone Star Office, Washington, Texas, 1852). Hereafter cited as Baptist State Convention Minutes, pp. 10-11.

[37]**Ibid.**, p. 7.

[38]Minutes, Jan. 22, 1852, p. 63.

[39]Hosea Garrett's Subscription Book (Baylor at Independence Papers, Texas Collection, Baylor University).

[40]Minutes, June 11, 1852, p. 69.

[41]Minutes, July 6, 1852, p. 74.

[42]Minutes, Dec. 16, 1852, p. 71.

[43]Minutes, July 5, 1852, p. 73.

period was from the last part of December to March 1, 1855.[44]

The collegiate class of the male department consisted of 15 scholars with 2 students comprising the junior class, 9 sophomores, and 4 freshmen. Eighty-six students were enrolled in the preparatory school making a total enrollment of 101 young men.[45] No mention was made of the enrollment in the female department, but in a letter to Judge Baylor, Burleson stated that there were one hundred eighty students in both departments which would indicate an enrollment of about seventy-nine girls.[46] Of the total enrollment only seven or eight young men were studying for the ministry.[47]

At least two of the goals set by the trustees in June of 1852 had been accomplished by the end of 1854: two small houses had been erected as dormitories,[48] and a set of laws and regulations had been drawn up and printed.[49] A portion of the laws defined the powers and duties of the Board of Trustees as well as the duties of the president and professors. The duties of the Board of Trustees were twofold: to enact the laws of the school, and to maintain a general supervision of the university. The trustees elected the professors, determined their salaries and could remove any professor from his position. The Board was completely in charge of the finance of the school through which they provided needed buildings and equipment, and fixed the rates of tuition.[50]

As president of the university, Burleson presided over all faculty meetings, voting only in cases of a tie. The president was the chief executor of the laws and could suspend any student, but only the trustees had the power of expulsion. Besides teaching a full schedule Burleson conducted the religious services held each morning and evening, maintained an account of each student's academic standing, sent a monthly report to the parents, and presented a semi-annual report to the trustees.[51]

Each professor was admonished to consider himself an officer of discipline as well as an instructor, carefully observing

---

[44]Catalogue, 1854, p. 16.
[45]**Ibid.**, pp. 3-5.
[46]Letter from R. C. Burleson to R. E. B. Baylor, April 7, 1854 (R. C. Burleson Papers, Texas Collection, Baylor University).
[47]Letter from R. C. Burleson to Richard Burleson, Feb. 6, 1854 (R. C. Burleson Papers, Texas Collection, Baylor University).
[48]Minutes, Dec. 21, 1854, p. 89.
[49]**Laws of the Baylor University, Independence, Washington County, Texas** (Austin: J. W. Hampton, 1854).
[50]**Ibid.** p. 3.
[51]**Ibid.**, p. 4.

any violation of the laws in class or elsewhere and reporting to the president. After each class period the teacher gave a numerical grade to each of his students, and on each Monday presented to the president a report of the standing of every student for the preceding week.[52]

In spite of a bad cotton crop yielding low prices, the trustees managed to keep the school's finances in good order.[53] Burleson and Professor J. B. Stiteler were paid out of the president's endowment, and the salaries of S. G. O'Bryan and B. S. Fitzgerald were paid out of monies received from tuition. The property value of the university was estimated to be about $40,000, and enrollment was still increasing despite the financial condition of the state.[54] Although the school was able to pay salaries, hard cash was not readily available. Burleson was forced to write Judge Baylor and ask for financial aid in the matter of a debt owed a William Norriss. In his letter Burleson informed the judge that he owed Norriss $50 but did not "have a dime in the world." Burleson requested Judge Baylor to pay the rest of the subscription to Norriss as partial payment of the debt.[55] Judge Baylor complied with the beleaguered presidents' request and paid Norriss $20.[56]

Even though handicapped with financial difficulties Burleson still maintained enough faith in the future of the university to write to his brother, Richard, in Alabama and offer him a position as professor in the male department. As an encouragement to Richard, he painted a glowing verbal picture of Texas and the school, giving the enrollment as "not far from 250 students" instead of the 180 actually enrolled. Burleson informed his brother that he had a fine, large home of seven rooms which could accommodate Richard and his family until they found adequate lodging. Burleson enthusiastically predicted that in ten years Texas would be the "New York of the South and Baylor University the higtest (*sic*) armament of Texas."[57]

By 1855 Baylor University was past the experimental stage and was regarded as one of the "fixed institutions in the coun-

---

[52]**Ibid.**, pp. 4-5.

[53]Baptist State Convention Minutes, 1855, p. 21.

[54]Baptist State Convention Minutes, 1854, p. 13.

[55]Letter from R. C. Burleson to R. E. B. Baylor, April 7, 1854 (R. C. Burleson Papers, Texas Collection, Baylor University).

[56]Receipt signed by Norriss (R. C. Burleson Papers, Texas Collection, Baylor University).

[57]Letter from R. C. Burleson to Richard Burleson, February 6, 1854 (R. C. Burleson Papers, Texas Collection, Baylor University).

try."[58] The school year began on March 1, 1855, with an enrollment of 25 boys in the collegiate department and 83 in the male preparatory department. The female department enrolled about 91 young ladies during the school year.[59] The male department increased to 230 scholars by December, 40 of whom were in the collegiate department.[60]

There were several important events during the 1855 school year. Growing public dissatisfaction with the institution prompted Stephen Decatur Rowe, a student at Baylor, to write an article for the *Texas Baptist* in which he replied to the many slanderous rumors going about concerning the poor standards of the university. Claims were being made to the effect that Baylor University graduates would not be received in sophomore classes of institutions in other states. Rowe emphatically defended his school and urged all Baptists to support the institution.[61]

The university not only received criticism but some praise as well. Many Baptists in Texas were proud of their institution and expressed confidence in the trustees who believed that nature had conferred the right of intellectual culture upon all and had placed the means within the reach of all who desired instruction.[62]

Late in 1854 Sam Houston had become an active patron of the school, offering the use of his "large and well selected library,"[63] contributing several valuable public documents,[64] and in April of 1855 he contributed $330 for the education of ministers.[65]

Two important administrative changes were made by the trustees in 1855; beginning in 1856 the male and female departments would publish separate catalogues,[66] and both Burleson and Clark were requested to each present an annual report to the Board stating the numbers of teachers employed, salaries

[58]Haynes, "Dr. Rufus C. Burleson," p. 54.
[59]Catalogue, 1855, pp. 3-4.
[60]**Washington American** (Washington, Texas), Dec. 14, 1855.
[61]**Texas Baptist** (Anderson, Texas), April 4, 1855.
[62]**Ibid.**
[63]Baptist State Convention Minutes, 1854, p. 13.
[64]Minutes, Oct. 18, 1854, p. 86.
[65]Minutes, April 10, 1855, p. 92.
[66]Minutes, Dec. 21, 1855, p. 100. However only in the 1851 catalogue was information given for both departments. In the male department catalogues from 1852-1856 a short paragraph was included which stated that the female department's catalogue was published separately. The first printed catalogue for the female department of which there is any knowledge was published in 1857, and there is no evidence to indicate catalogues were printed before 1857.

they received, the enrollment and total amount of tuition collected.[67] Thus, by 1855 Burleson and Clark and their departments were beginning to go their separate ways with each man working toward the advancement of his respective charges.

By the end of 1855 the trustees were able to announce that the sum of $5,000 had been raised for the purpose of erecting a suitable building to house the female department, and a contractor had been engaged to begin construction. The female department had succeeded in spite of the disadvantages incurred by Burleson, and the performance of required duties was becoming a drain upon Clark's resources. The trustees hoped that another person could soon be procured to take over the boarding house so that Clark would be released from serving tables.[68]

In December of 1855 Burleson and Clark were able to confer the first degrees in the history of the university with Stephen Decatur Rowe[69] and Mary Gentry Kavanaugh[70] constituting the first graduating class.

Early in the 1856 school year tragedy struck the Burleson home with the birth and death of a daughter on May 10.[71] In spite of his personal loss Burleson wrote Richard glowing reports of conditions at Independence. Since he was trying to persuade his brother to come to Baylor and teach, the facts were at times exaggerated. He wrote an encouraging report of his financial condition, $2,000 from tuition, $600 for preaching, $800 from the endowment, totaling $3,400.[72] To this amount could be added the income from the boarders of which he had from eight to ten.[73] In fact Burleson's financial condition was so good that he began the construction of a "splendid house on the College lot."[74] This was the octagonal house which was used throughout the remaining years of Baylor at Independence.

Not only were the finances of the president in good order, but those of the university as well. Perhaps one reason for this fact was the efficient manner in which the trustees began to collect the subscriptions when they became due. The school

---

[67]Minutes, June 19, 1855, p. 94.
[68]Minutes of the Baptist State Convention, 1855, p. 22.
[69]Catalogue, 1855, p. 3.
[70]Riley, **History of Texas Baptists,** p. 132.
[71]Letter from R. C. Burleson to Richard Burleson, May 11, 1856 (R. C. Burleson Papers, Texas Collection, Baylor University).
[72]Letter from R. C. Burleson to Richard Burleson, Sept. 16, 1856 (R. C. Burleson Papers, Texas Collection, Baylor University).
[73]Letter from R. C. Burleson to Richard Burleson, Oct. 1, 1856 (R. C. Burleson Papers, Texas Collection, Baylor University).
[74]Letter from R. C. Burleson to Richard Burleson, Sept. 16, 1856.

had begun to use a printed request form thereby eliminating the necessity of the treasurer or an agent personally contacting every subscriber.

Independence, Texas Nov. 25, 1856

Dear Sir:

I am happy to inform you that our University, to which you have generously contributed, is in a flourishing condition, one hundred and fifty students have been matriculated during this year.

Our President and four Professors are all at the post of duty, and are toiling by day and by night to sustain this great enterprise.

The year, however, draws to a close, when their salaries will be due.

I therefore, by appointment of the Trustees wish to inform you that the sum of............................now due, is greatly needed.

Will you, therefore, send the amount by mail at our risk, or retain it till called on by an agent?

Yours truly,
G. W. Graves
Treasurer of the Endowment Fund[75]

At the close of the 1856 school year the male collegiate department conferred degrees upon six young men giving a total of eight graduates endowed with a degree from Baylor University.[76]

1857 was indeed a year of progress for the university! In spite of a statewide crop failure, the enrollment was as good as ever.[77] By the end of December the male department had five candidates for degrees, a senior class of 4, a junior class of 14, 13 sophomores, and 16 freshmen. In addition there were 34 enrolled in a scientific course of study. The preparatory school had the largest enrollment in its existence—121—bringing the total male student body at 207.[78]

With six professors and teachers and about one hundred pupils in regular attendance the female department was well on its way toward matching the male department in importance. The new college edifice was completed, and a new set of pianos as well as philosophical and chemical apparatus had been pur-

---

[75]Printed request (Baylor at Independence Papers, Texas Collection, Baylor University).

[76]Catalogue, 1856-1857, p. 5.

[77]Baptist State Convention Minutes, 1858, p. 18.

[78]Catalogue, 1856-1857, pp. 5-12.

chased.[79] By 1857 the female department had become so popular that many local people urged the addition of an elementary level preparatory school for females so that other girls could acquire the training necessary for admission to the school.[80] In December of 1857 fourteen girls had completed the required course of study necessary for graduation.[81]

In January of 1857 the *Texas Baptist* announced the publishing of the *Texas Literary Journal.* This journal was edited by the professors of Baylor and contained subjects purely literary, "entirely neutral, and on religion and politics." Special attention would be given to the best methods of organizing and disciplining schools and colleges, geology, botany, zoology, mineralogy, ornithology, and historical subjects.[82] Thus having finally attained the respectability of success the school and its teachers now felt in a position to advise and lend the wisdom of their experiences to other aspiring scholars and institutions.

In the summer of 1857 the trustees proudly announced the organization of a law school.[83] A voluntary faculty composed of R. T. Wheeler, R. E. B. Baylor, and W. P. Rogers conducted the classes with the object of establishing a plan of instruction on correct principles by which young men of Texas could enter the practice of law on equal terms with lawyers of other states. The first session began on June 15 and lasted through September. Students were required to attend two sessions before they obtained a Bachelor of Laws degree. Instruction consisted of the use of textbooks, daily examinations, lectures, and moot courts. The lectures were concerned with the different branches of legal science adapted to the laws of the time and the local jurisprudence of the state. Each session cost $36 for tuition, $5 for library fee, and $1 for incidental expenses. No previous professional reading or proficiency in classical literature was required for admission.[84] Therefore for about $84 and two summers of instruction, a young man could become a bona fide and degree-possessing lawyer. During the first session in the summer of 1857 thirteen students attended the lectures.[85]

In 1858 the university began to experience a new kind of

---

[79]Baptist State Convention Minutes, 1858, pp. 18-19.
[80]**Washington American** (Washington, Texas), March 19, 1857.
[81]Baptist State Convention Minutes, 1858, p. 18.
[82]**Texas Baptist** (Anderson, Texas), Jan. 7, 1857.
[83]**Ibid.**, June 10, 1857.
[84]Circular (Baylor at Independence Papers, Texas Collection, Baylor University).
[85]Baptist State Convention Minutes, 1858, p. 18.

problem—due to the large enrollments, the trustees faced the problem of inadequate buildings and equipment. With a total of 99 students in the male department one building and seven teachers were insufficient to meet the desired goals.[86] The female department with an enrollment of 113 students[87] and a new building was not as pressed as Burleson's department, but the new building still lacked adequate furnishings and apparatus.[88] To help alleviate the problem of furniture the Board asked the Independence Baptist Church, which used the new building for its services, to donate their benches on the condition that the church would not have to pay for the use of the building on Sundays.[89]

Burleson issued a plea for contributions of books, needing at least one thousand books added to the library by 1859. Some books were donated: a full set of "Gill's Commentaries" in nine volumes, Greenleaf's *Testimonies of the Gospels,* "Scott's Commentaries" in three voulmes, and a full set of "Henry's Commentaries," but the number of books hardly met Burleson's desired goal.[90]

By 1859 the population of Texas had increased rapidly in the western parts of the state, and Washington County was no longer the thriving community that it had once been. Instead the village was described as "unusually quiet and wears the sober appearance of an old town in one of the older states, where people feel themselves settled, and live there because they want to."[91] Many Baptists felt that the university should be moved to a more central and populous area. Agitation for such a move became so great that the trustees were forced to issue a statement on the subject:

> Resolved, that the Trustees do hereby declare that the removal of the university is both inconsistent with our charter, and impracticable, and we consider its location permanent and not debatable.[92]

This resolution left no doubt as to the intentions of the Board,

---

[86]Catalogue, 1858, pp. 4-11.

[87]Broadside (Baylor at Indeepndence Papers, Texas Collection, Baylor University).

[88]**Texas Baptist** (Anderson, Texas), Sept. 9, 1858.

[89]Minutes, June 16, 1858, p. 118.

[90]**Texas Baptist** (Anderson, Texas), Sept. 30, 1858.

[91]**Ibid.**, Sept. 9, 1858.

[92]Minutes, Dec. 1, 1858, p. 120.

but agitation continued until Baylor's move to Waco and Belton in 1885.[93]

Toward the end of the 1859 school year the university showed financial and academic improvement over the previous year. Three or four hundred volumes had been added to the library; approximately $1,200 had been raised in cash or subscriptions for needed apparatus of which about $500 worth had already been purchased and was being used, and $1,000 had been added to the endowment fund by selling land that had been donated to the school.[94] The university was valued at about $65,000, including buildings, lands, endowments, and subscriptions. Both departments totaled fourteen professors and teachers with an enrollment of 275 pupils.[95]

In 1859 the school year was changed from one term of ten months to two terms. The spring term began February 1 and ended July 1 with a vacation from July 1 to the end of August. The fall term was from September 1 to December 16 with two weeks off for Christmas. The 1860 spring term was scheduled to begin on January 2.[96] To provide room for the expanding institution, the trustees took action by granting a contract for the erection of a new stone building for the male department at a cost of $4,604.[97]

In the 1859 commencement exercises six young men[98] and one young lady[99] received degrees from the university. In a letter to his brother, Richard, Burleson indicated that the law school also graduated some sixteen aspiring lawyers.[100]

Although the university was prospering, Burleson was not. Poor health hindered his activities, and he was forced to travel to a better climate in Tennessee. Burleson never seemed to be able to maintain financial stability for very long, and 1859 was no exception. His brother urged him to get his finances in order before returning to Texas—"I hope, dear Rufus, that you not return to Texas without getting your money matters streaght-

---

[93]Link, **Historical and Biographical Magazine**, p. 469.

[94]Baptist State Convention Minutes, 1859, p. 10.

[95]**Report on the Legal Relations of Baylor University to the Baptist State Convention of Texas,** October, 1859, p. 5 (Baylor at Independence Papers, Texas Collection, Baylor University).

[96]Catalogue, 1859, p. 37.

[97]Baptist State Convention Minutes, 1859, p. 10.

[98]Portion of a letter in the R. C. Burleson Papers, Texas Collection, Baylor University.

[99]Catalogue, Female Department, 1859-1860, p. 7.

[100]Letter from R. C. Burleson to Richard Burleson, Sept. 15, 1859 (R. C. Burleson Papers, Texas Collection, Baylor University).

ened (*sic*) up. Let our friends and relations know your embarrassment, and I hope they will help you."[101]

While in Tennessee Burleson had been offered the presidency of Union University and several other more lucrative positions.[102] These offers he declined because he was dedicated to Texas and wished to continue his work there.[103]

For several years there had been a growing pride in the state convention concerning the accomplishments of the university. Along with this growing pride emerged an attitude that the school was the personal property of the Baptist State Convention. This feeling naturally created animosities and difficulties between the trustees and the convention, and by 1859 the conflicting views could no longer be ignored.

The convention appointed Clark, Burleson, Garrett, W. A. Montgomery, and C. P. Breedlove to report on the legal relations between the convention and the university. This committee reported to the convention that the trustees had the sole power to govern the school, and the only legal relation between the convention and the university was the power to fill vacancies in the Board. The committee continuing its report was quite blunt in condemnation of the attitude of the state convention:

> . . . your committee are unable to perceive upon what principle of law or reason this *Convention* can claim the right to exercise the privileges of founders and donors in respect to a charity, founded before she had an existence; and to which she never, as a Convention, has contributed one dollar.[104]

This report was printed as a separate pamphlet and was not included in the official minutes of the 1859 session.

1860 was a significant year in the history of Baylor University at Independence. In the space of one year Baylor reached its apex and then began a rapid decline. By 1860 Baylor University was well known in at least the Southern States and was catalogued by the *London Times* as one of the prominent institutions of learning in America.[105]

---

[101]Letter from Richard Burleson to R. C. Burleson, Sept. 15, 1859 (R. C. Burleson Papers, Texas Collection, Baylor University).

[102]**Texas Baptist Herald** (Houston), Dec. 1, 1859.

[103]Letter from R. C. Burleson to Union University, Aug. 22, 1859 (R. C. Burleson Papers, Texas Collection, Baylor University).

[104]**Report of the Legal Relation Between Baylor University and the Baptist State Convention of Texas.**

[105]Haynes, "Dr. Rufus C. Burleson," p. 54.

Under the leadership of Mr. and Mrs. Clark the female department had surpassed the male department in accomplishments. They had acquired a fine new building three stories in height, and a library had been begun by the voluntary contributions of the young ladies and friends of the school. The library was also furnished with subscriptions to several standard periodicals plus some of the newspapers in the state. With an enrollment of over 150, a staff of nine professors and teachers and $1,200 of recently purchased apparatus, the department enjoyed "a great degree of prosperity."[106]

The male department also had a large enrollment, and the prospects for a good year were high. In August of 1860 General Sam Houston addressed the students of the male department. He expressed a strong and increasing attachment to Baylor, "as one of the oldest and most successful colleges in the state . . ." Houston stated his belief in wholesome discipline and submission to law as being indispensable to the education of youth, and that no institution could succeed without firm discipline. The General also indicated that he was against the establishing of a state university, preferring rather to endow the institutions already established. In conclusion Houston expressed a desire to see Baylor permanently endowed.[107]

Baylor's finances were in good order, and Burleson and his faculty received a total of $7,697.62 in salaries from the Board.[108] In June the faculty of the male department recommended that honorary degrees of A.M. or *Secundum Gradum* be conferred upon James H. Stribling, Professor James L. Smith, and Professor O. H. Leland.[109]

Even as the school prospered storm clouds of despair were gathering, and the ensuing deluge of troubles would all but finish the then prospering school. The year even had an ominous beginning with an epidemic of yellow fever which caused hundreds of deaths.[110] The coming presidential election and the prospects of war undoubtedly had a tremendous effect upon the students and faculty of the university, but the crisis which would have the greatest effect upon the school, the community, and the denomination—the feud between Burleson and Clark—was

---

[106]Baptist State Convention Minutes, 1860, p. 23.
[107]**Texas Baptist** (Anderson, Texas), Aug. 2, 1860.
[108]Minutes, Jan. 10, 1861, p. 155.
[109]Minutes, June 27, 1860.
[110]Letter from H. B. Carroll to Col. J. C. Barrow, Jan. 7, 1860 (Baylor at Independence Papers, Texas Collection, Baylor University).

rapidly coming to a head and would soon overshadow all other problems. In one year the university reached its greatest prosperity only to be plunged into despair and almost ruination.

4

The Burleson-Clark Feud

ACCORDING to Burleson, the feud began in 1854,[1] but hard feelings more than likely began in 1851. From the start of their association Burleson seemed to hold the attitude that the male department and its functions were of primary importance; the female department was in all ways secondary to the male department. Before Burleson accepted the presidency he insisted that the males and females be separated in all academic activities. Another indication of his favoritism toward the male department was the fact that he moved his department to the new stone edifice, leaving the old and decayed wooden academy building for Clark and his girls.[2] Technically Burleson was in charge of both departments, but he devoted his time and energy exclusively to the male department, and as long as the female department did not interfere with the functions of his department Burleson was willing to let Clark have a free hand. This slighting attitude upon the part of Burleson from the beginning constituted grounds for unkind thoughts from Clark.

Precious little provocation was needed in those days to spur the Baptist brethren to action. This quickness to take offense is illustrated by an anecdote related by Z. N. Morrell. In the second meeting of the Education Society R. E. B. Baylor refused to return Morrell's greeting. Morrell in return acted indifferently toward Baylor. Later on during the session Baylor rose before the group and apologized for his behavior, explaining that he had mistaken Morrell for a man named Merrill who had been excluded from the Lord's Supper by Huckins who was then pastor of the Houston church. After this explanation Baylor and Morrell were quickly reconciled.[3]

[1]Carroll, **Texas Baptists,** p. 240.

[2]**Supra,** p. 38.

[3]Morrell, **Fruits and Flowers,** pp. 138-139.

Clark and Burleson differed greatly in character and manner. Burleson, a young man, was ambitious and worked tirelessly toward promoting himself and the university. Burleson wrote to Richard and explained that he was chosen president of the university not because of his superiority but because of his vigilance and untiring energy. "I have traversed the whole state and know every prominent person in our church."[4]

Clark, an older man, was also ambitious; he worked for the improvement and success of his department, but he did it in a quieter and more dignified manner congruous to his nature.

With both men working diligently for the advancement of their respective charges, trouble between Clark and Burleson was inevitable. From 1851 to 1857 the friction increased until even the Board of Trustees came to the realization that an "unpleasant state of feeling" existed. A committee was appointed to investigate the rumor.[5]

The committee discovered that the "rumor" was true and reported that the differences were over the internal government of the institution.[6] The Board rapidly sought to eliminate further trouble over the manner in which the departments were conducted by separating the two departments. Burleson would no longer be responsible for the female department.[7] The Board quickly informed both men who really controlled the school by stating its right to scrutinize and judge every rule and regulation and to correct anything detrimental to the interests of the pupils or the institution. The Board further stated that it also had the right to supervise and control the entire institution which meant both departments.[8] Under pressure from the Board, Burleson and Clark came to a "free and full explanation of all difficulties, and gave hands in a pledge of cordial cooperation."[9] As far as the Board was concerned the matter was settled once and for all.

The matter, however, was not settled in Burleson's mind. There is much to indicate that jealousy was the crux of the entire trouble. As the female department achieved more and more success, the friction increased. Seeing this success, Bur-

---

[4]Letter from R. C. Burleson to Richard Burleson, Feb. 6, 1854 (R. C. Burleson Papers, Texas Collection, Baylor University).

[5]Minutes, Dec. 16, 1857, p. 113.

[6]Minutes, Dec. 18, 1857, p. 115.

[7]**Ibid.**, p. 114.

[8]**Ibid.**, p. 116.

[9]**Ibid.**, p. 117.

leson asserted his legal rights as president and began to take an active interest in the affairs of Clark's department. Although Burleson was within his rights, Clark naturally resented the interference. Clark had made a success of the female department in spite of Burleson's attitude. The crowning achievement of Clark's efforts came in 1857 with the completion of a new building much larger and better equipped than Burleson's building. Clark was the designer, building committee, supervising architect, and solicitor for the funds—the building came about through his efforts without much help from the Board and with none from Burleson.[10] When Burleson began to dictate to Clark he naturally considered this action unfair. The trustees realized the justification of Clark's disagreement with Burleson, and for this reason they removed the president's authority over the female department. This was a great blow to Burleson's ego, and the matter was not settled as far as he was concerned.

Agitation on the part of Burleson continued through 1858. The professors and students influenced by their respect for Burleson, also entered the affray. Some, like D. R. Wallace, were very outspoken in their opinions of Clark. The trouble between Wallace and Clark finally came to the attention of the trustees who requested both men to appear before the Board. After listening to Clark's explanation the Board requested Wallace to apologize which he did, after which Clark and Wallace "parted with mutual understanding."[11] Nor could the Board ignore Burleson's constant grumblings; so he, too, was summoned before the trustees and "a free and full interchange of opinion was had with Pres. Burleson, touching matters with him and the Trustees . . ." Both parties agreed to forget all differences and pledged cooperation. Burleson led in the closing prayer, and the "right hand of fellowship" was extended.[12] Again the trustees felt that they had settled the matter.

However, it became apparent that not only had the trouble not been settled, it had increased to dangerous proportions. This time it was Clark who opened with the first broadside. In February of 1860, R. T. Wheeler resigned from his position in the law school and opened his own school in Brenham. Burleson

---

[10]Horace Clark Scrapbook (Texas Collection, Baylor University).
[11]Minutes, Dec. 4, 1858, p. 127.
[12]**Ibid.**, pp. 126-127.

and his faculty were very critical of Wheeler's action, but Clark sided with the lawyer. Clark sent an article supporting Wheeler's action to George W. Baines, editor of the *Texas Baptist*, who printed it anonymously.[13] Burleson somehow found out that Clark was the author. This situation angered Burleson since he felt that Clark was meddling in something that was none of his affair. Burleson had also submitted an article to Baines requesting that it be printed under Baines' name or under the name of the denomination; this Baines had refused to do.[14] After Clark's letter, opinions came from all sides, and an active newspaper controversy ensued.[15] Thus was the feud begun again with renewed vigor and promise of dire consequences.

Early in June of 1860 Burleson wrote a letter to Baines stating his desire to end the troubles so that "as Baptists we may present an individual front,"[16] but feelings had progressed beyond the point of retraction. The inevitable clash occurred on Sunday, June 17, 1860, during the evening service of the Independence Baptist Church, of which both Clark and Burleson were members. During the meeting Judge Baylor made reference to "dissensions and jealousies in the Church," after which Burleson arose and said that he had felt the "fraternal dagger." He dramatically told the congregation that "while kneeling by the grave of his mother, he had resolved by the grace of God, never to criminate or recriminate any further than was necessary to vindicate his character." Clark then arose and told the assembly that "it was needless to affect ignorance of the insinuations of Pres't Burleson." Clark stated emphatically that he had striven for peace year after year, even going so far as to write a letter to Burleson inviting him to meet with Clark in his office at any time Burleson chose. Since Burleson had refused his offer, Clark felt that he was not responsible for the existing difficulties. Burleson again arose and told the members that he refused Clark's offer because Clark had not come to him as the Gospel required but had summoned him to his office. Burleson also indicated that Clark's letter had charged him with insincerity and hypocrisy, which

---

[13]Letter from Horace Clark to George Baines, June 18, 1860 (Horace Clark Papers, Texas Collection, Baylor University).

[14]**Ibid.**

[15]Letter from George Baines to Horace Clark, Aug. 10, 1860 (Horace Clark Papers, Texas Collection, Baylor University).

[16]Letter from R. C. Burleson to George Baines, June 3, 1860 (Baines Papers, Texas Collection, Baylor University).

Burleson felt placed "a wall of fire" between them until the charges were retracted.[17]

After the letter was sent, Burleson and the male department were further angered when Clark refused to allow the girls to attend the public monthly exercise of the senior class or the commencement party. Some of the seniors requested Burleson to announce a meeting after one of the chapel services, and Burleson made the announcement without knowing the nature of the meeting. After the students were assembled, he asked two of the senior boys about the meeting. When told that the boys were going to discuss Clark's action, Burleson suggested that they not hold the meeting. But since the young men replied that feeling would be worse if they did not go ahead with the discussion, Burleson allowed the meeting to be held. A formal protest was drawn up and presented to the Board of Trustees. In the face of this action Clark relented. Now the girls got into the affray—angered at such treatment of their beloved principal, they circulated a petition which forbade the signer to go to the boys' party, and a "young lady of Mr. Clark's family" wrote to her beau informing him that she would have nothing to do with him unless he stopped condemning Clark's actions.[18]

Once again the Board of Trustees was forced to take action. On June 27, the trustees drew up a statement, and a copy was sent to both men:

> Whereas it is evident that an unpleasant state of feeling exists between Eld. R. C. Burleson President of this Institution and Elder H. Clark principal of the female department, and whereas said Controversy is operating injuriously to both departments, be therefore Resolved, That we ignore anything which may have transpired between those brethren previous to Dec. 1857 at which time an adjustment of all difficulties then existing (between?) them took place in this Board. And that we request and expect those brethren to make all laudable efforts to adjust all matters of controversy generated since the above date, and submit said settlement to this board at 8 O'Clock Saturday morning.
>
> And in case they fail fail to do this, they will be expected to lay before us all of their aggrievances in writing for our adjustment, and if either of the above requests are

[17]**Defense of Abner E. Lipscomb,** 1860. Hereafter cited as Lipscomb Pamphlet (Baylor at Independence Papers, Texas Collection, Baylor University), p. 11.

[18]Lipscomb Pamphlet, p. 13.

> (not?) complied with, we request their resignations, as this injurious state of things must cease.[19]

On June 29, Burleson and Clark appeared before the Board and told the trustees that they had not settled their differences. Each man presented a written statement of his grievances and departed.[20] The combatants again came before the Board on June 30. At this time each read his charges, offered proof, and made speeches to sustain them.

Burleson presented six charges against Clark: (1) Clark on June 17 publicly charged him with being the cause of the dissensions and party strife in the Independence Church; (2) Clark had revived the differences of 1857; (3) Clark had written a letter charging him with insincerity and hypocrisy and charging family and friends with crimes that made him "sick at heart;" (4) Clark treated Mrs. Burleson and him with disrespect by not allowing the daughters of friends and brethren to meet a few select people at his house; (5) Clark used his official position in a speech before the female department during school hours to prejudice "young and unsuspecting minds against me." Burleson demanded that these charges against him be proven or withdrawn publicly; (6) Burleson felt grieved that Clark had interfered with the management of the male department by vindicating and endorsing Wheeler's resignation as head of the law department and his opening of a law school in Brenham.[21]

After Burleson's charges were read, Clark told the Board that the reason he did not allow the girls to accept Burleson's invitation was because the female teachers in his department were not invited to accompany the girls as was the general custom.[22] As for the letter so prominent in Burleson's argument, Clark told the Board that it was "kind and Christian." When the Board asked Burleson to produce the letter, he informed them that he could not find it.[23]

Clark then presented his grievances against Burleson: (1) Burleson had compelled him to arise in a religious assembly "to reply to what I and others conceived to be a personal attack upon me;" (2) Burleson permitted a disrespectful demonstration

---

[19]Written copy (Baylor at Independence Papers, Texas Collection, Baylor University).

[20]Minutes, June 29, 1860, p. 144.

[21]Minutes, June 30, 1860, pp. 145-146.

[22]Notation (Baylor at Independence Papers, Texas Collection, Baylor University).

[23]Lipscomb Pamphlet, pp. 15-16.

toward him on the part of the students of the male department; (3) Burleson circulated a letter written to him by Clark and used it to place Clark in the attitude of an aggressor; (4) Burleson publicly made "disparaging remarks" concerning the female department; (5) Burleson was unwilling to submit differences to the arbitration of mutual friends; (6) Burleson was not willing to settle differences upon a mutually honorable basis.[24]

After both men had their say, the Board requested them to retire while they deliberated upon what action to take.[25] That evening the Board informed Burleson and Clark of its decisions. As to Burleson's charges against Clark, the trustees had nothing to say about the first two charges. Concerning the third charge the trustees requested Clark to withdraw the remarks made in the letter. In the matter about the party the Board felt that Clark's explanation was enough. As to the fifth charge the Board sustained the charge that Clark did address his department over the differences, but the trustees felt that his address did not have a prejudicial effect against the male department. The trustees did disapprove of Clark's letter to the *Texas Baptist* concerning Wheeler, but they believed that Clark had no designs of reflecting on the faculty of the male department.[26]

The Board was not as lenient with Burleson; the trustees condemned his actions on June 17; they disapproved of his conduct in regard to the meeting after chapel, and of his remarks in regard to the female department. The Board also disapproved of Burleson's refusals to take the matter to mutual friends for settlement.[27]

On July 1, 1860, the Board, its patience at an end, prepared a formal statement of its decisions as well as other pronouncements. With both men present the statement was read: (1) Clark was to withdraw his letter, and the Board did not want to hear any more about it; (2) neither party was compromising their honor as Christian gentlemen in accepting the adjustments proposed by the Board; (3) Clark was requested to publish a letter in the *Texas Baptist* thereby showing that his other letter contained no intentional disrespect to the faculty of the male department; (4) if either of the men again were part of or

[24]Minutes, June 30, 1860, p. 144.
[25]**Ibid.**, p. 146.
[26]Minutes, June 30, 1860 (Evening meeting), p. 144.
[27]**Ibid.**, p. 147.

condoned a demonstration of disrespect by one department against another the Board would invoke the highest penalty known in the charter or by-laws; (5) the Board felt that all adjustments were fair and impartial, and that both parties should make a public announcement of a settlement at the Baptist meeting house that evening after preaching; (6) since the controversy was ruinous to the institution the Board considered this the final settlement and no other compromises would be considered—" . . . let it be known that our patience with their petty difficulties is *exhausted* and for the future no compromises will be required but we shall with the fear of God before our eyes promptly apply the remedy even if it should sever the ties that connect us together from President to the last professor if they shall merit it by their conduct;" (7) the Board considered the adjustments made honorable and reasonable to all concerned, and the president, principal, and professors were requested to signify their cooperation; (8) it was finally resolved that public notice was to be given through the *Texas Baptist* that all difficulties had been adjusted satisfactorily. Hosea Garrett, President of the Board of Trustees, called upon Clark and Burleson to agree to the settlement which they did.[28]

Not everyone felt that the decisions of the Board had been fair and impartial. One of the local men, Abner E. Lipscomb, acting as proxy for the trustee, A. C. Horton, during the June 29-July 1 sessions, felt that the Board had been grossly unfair to Burleson. He refused to vote in the affirmative on several of the decisions which were otherwise unanimous. After receiving much criticism for his stand, Lipscomb published a pamphlet in which he defended his actions.[29] The majority of the Baptists around Independence seemed to have sided with the trustees and Clark. When Lipscomb arose before the church and made charges against Clark, the congregation refused to sustain them. When Lipscomb refused to accept their decision he was removed from the fellowship of the church. Later in July, 1861, Lipscomb came before the church and not only withdrew his charges but renounced his pamphlet as well, thereby gaining acceptance back into the fold.[30]

Although Burleson and Clark had come to a settlement and seemed willing to leave it at that, people in the town kept the

[28]Minutes, July 1, 1860, pp. 149-51.
[29]Lipscomb Pamphlet.
[30]Printed Report (Baylor at Independence Papers, Texas Collection, Baylor University).

issue alive and threatened to do much damage to all concerned.[31] Because of this the Board of Trustees was forced to find out if the trouble was beginning anew. Both Clark and Burleson assured the Board that they had not violated the Board's decision, which they were willing to abide by.[32] The trustees felt that a verbal denial of the existence of trouble was not sufficient; so a written statement was prepared, and each member of the faculty was requested to sign it:

> We the President and Professors of Baylor University and Principal of the Female Department certify that
>
> Whereas reports are in circulation that our relations in the above capacity as professors are not of a friendly character
>
> These reports are unfounded, since the adjustment of difficulties by the Board of Trustees last July, we have had no cause for a renewal of those feelings which unfortunately had existed, and we do solemnly pledge ourselves for the future that while we hold our present connection with the University, we will do or say nothing directly or indirectly to disturb the friendly and peaceable relations between us as professors of the department or the Board of Trustees.
>
> Rufus C. Burleson
> Richard B. Burleson
> D. R. Wallace
> O. H. Leland
> Geo. W. Willric
> H. Clark
> B. S. Fitzgerald[33]

On March 21, 1861, R. C. Burleson, Richard B. Burleson, D. R. Wallace, and O. H. Leland gave formal notice of their intention to "withdraw their connection with the University at the end of the present session." The Board accepted the notice and immediately began plans for filling the vacancies.[34]

This action on the part of the male department's president and faculty probably did not come as a surprise to the trustees. As early as 1860 Burleson had expressed a desire to exchange his house and lots on the campus for wild lands belonging to the school.[35] In February, 1861, Burleson sent the Board a

---

[31]Letter from James L. Farquhar to J. W. Barnes, April 1, 1861 (Baylor at Independence Papers, Texas Collection, Baylor University).

[32]Minutes, March 20, 1861, p. 156.

[33]**Ibid.**

[34]Minutes, March 21, 1861, pp. 158-159.

[35]Minutes, November ?, 1860, pp. 151-152.

memorandum which indicated that he and his faculty were at least contemplating a move:

> Feb. 26, 1861
> We the President and Professors of the Male Department of Baylor do hereby enter into the articles of agreement
> 1st We pledge ourselves to cooperate together to build up a great and flourishing Institution at some eligible point in Texas.
> 2nd The basis of cooperation to be our present relations in this Institution.
> 3rd To secure these ends (in?) view more certainly to promise to aid, defend and sustain each to the utmost of our ability.
> 4th In all matters of interest the will of the majority to rule
> 5th In the present difficulties before the Trustees in regard to H. Clark we will stand or fall, stay or go together
> 6th We will remain here as teachers or go to Waco or elsewhere as the will of the majority of our number will decide
> 7th We will do all in our power in accordance with justice to promote the pecuniary social and professional interest of each member of this Faculty[36]

On November 10, 1860, the Waco Association was organized, and the Trinity River Association School in Waco was adopted by the new association which changed the name to the Waco Classical School.[37] In January of 1861 the president of the school's board of trustees was authorized to correspond with Burleson and his faculty and try to get them to take over the Waco school.[38]

The trustees of Baylor, their patience already exhausted, were not unduly alarmed at the prospect of losing Burleson and his faculty. J. L. Farquhar expressed the true sentiments of the Board in a "burn this!" letter. Farquhar requested the recipient to keep the information to himself "and never express any anxiety for them to leave though we would be much gratified if they would." "I think we should be very cautious and not let them know we are favorable to the removal of the last

[36] Memorandum (Baylor at Independence Papers, Texas Collection, Baylor University).
[37] Carroll, **Texas Baptists,** p. 224.
[38] **Minutes of Waco** University and Classical School, January 21, 1861 (Texas Collection, Baylor University).

one of the Male Department of Baylor University from Independence."[39]

On May 16 the trustees began action toward securing a new president and faculty. A committee was appointed and instructed to secure suitable persons to take charge of the male department. The Board resolved to guarantee the new president an annual salary of $2,000 and the professors were to receive $1,200.[40]

A letter addressed to the Board was received from Burleson who assured the trustees that he and the faculty had the "deepest affection and kindest remembrance" toward those with whom there were differences, and that no unkind feelings were harbored. The Board in reply assured Burleson that the trustees' desire for the separation was influenced only by "brotherly love and affection."[41]

In June and July of 1861 the trustees went about the task of making final arrangements with the departing faculty, and of trying to get everything ready for the 1862 school year. On June 26, Burleson informed the Board that $621.78 in the possession of the male department would be kept. He felt that the money was due him since it had been obtained only through his efforts. There was no recorded response from the Board.[42]

On June 28 the president and faculty of the male department submitted their formal resignations which were accepted by the Board.[43]

On June 29 Garrett sent a note to Burleson requesting the reasons why the male department had not held its commencement and examination exercises. Burleson sent the trustees a lengthy reply:

1. The Civil War which has suspended most of the best endowed colleges in the South.
2. A local war was threatened between some of the citizens of this place and our students.
3. You advised me to adjourn the University rather than have an outbreak so seriously threatened.
4. The Senior Class, the largest we ever had informed us in writing that they had determined not to present themselves for Graduation, but will apply for, and no doubt

[39]Letter from James L. Farquhar to ?, April 27, 1861 (Baylor at Independence Papers, Texas Collection, Baylor University).
[40]Minutes, May 16, 1861, p. 161.
[41]**Ibid.**, pp. 160-161.
[42]Minutes, Juune 26, 1861,p. 163.
[43]Minutes, June 28, 1861,pp. 163-164.

> receive their Diplomas from Waco University on the 4th of Sept. 1861. . . .[44]

On July 17, from the recommendation of the appointed committee, George W. Baines was elected as President and Professor of Natural Science; S. G. O'Brien was elected Professor of Mathematics, and John C. Anderson was elected Professor of Ancient and Modern Languages. At Baines' request his salary was fixed at $1,500 annually while the professors' salaries remained $1,200.[45]

Although Burleson and his department were about ready to leave for their new positions at Waco University, several items had not been settled to the satisfaction of the trustees; so a committee was chosen to make the necessary adjustments. The Board informed Burleson that failure to make satisfactory settlement could cause irritation and misrepresentations.[46] Rumors were abroad that the students and faculty were planning to take most of the books and apparatus with them; so Richard Burleson asked the trustees to straighten out the matter.[47] The Board replied that although the trustees had approved the removal of some apparatus, there was no way to determine whether or not books had also been taken.[48] Thus even to the last, relations were strained due to distrust and ill feeling from both sides.

The ill feeling between Clark and Burleson did not end with Burlesons' move to Waco but continued for many years. In 1885 when Clark delivered the baccalaureate address at Baylor at Belton, Burleson, being present sought him out and offered to shake hands and "bury the hatchet" which Clark did.[49]

In his memoirs Judge Baylor summed up the trouble between Clark and Burleson very well:

> But unfortunately these two good brethren differed in the manner of conducting our literary institutions. This difference of opinion brought them into collission (*sic*) and worked most disastrously for the prosperity of our beloved

[44]Minutes, June 29, 1861,pp.165, 167-168.
[45]Minutes, July 17, 1861, pp. 166-167.
[46]Minutes, July 27, 1851, p. 170.
[47]Letter from Richard Burleson to the Board of Trustees, July 19, 1861 (Baylor at Independence Papers, Texas Collection, Baylor University).
[48]Letter from the Board of Trustees to Richard Burleson, July 26, 1861 (Baylor at Independence Papers, Texas Collection, Baylor University).
[49]Letter from Horace Clark Jr. to Herbert Gambrell, Dec. 14, 1835 (Horace Clark Papers, Texas Collection, Baylor University).

> institution. I believe they are now both fully satisfied of this fact. . . .
>
> How much better would it have been for these brothers to have only an amicable difference of opinion.
>
> That they both erred I do not doubt for a moment and I believe each of them begins to look at the past in this light. May they both live to forget and forgive all that has ever transpired between them is the Prayer of their mutual friend and brother.[50]

Even though torn with internal strife, and experiencing the first effects of the beginning Civil War, the trustees reported to the Baptist State Convention their plans for continuing the sixteen-year-old institution:

> Baylor University, in common with similar institutions of the country, is suffering on account of the present national troubles through which we are passing. Youth and young men have generally joined the army in defence of the liberties and rights of our Government; and whereas others are yet left at home, the unprecedented money crisis will, in many cases prevent their entering college. Since the last meeting of the Convention, the Board has found it necessary to furnish a new faculty for the Male Department occasioned by the resignation of the former faculty, which took effect at the close of the last session. This the Trustees did by electing for one year Elder G. W. Baines, A.M. President and Professor of Natural Science, Elder J. F. Hillyer, M.D., A.M., Professor Mathematics, and J. C. Anderson, A.M., Professor Modern and Ancient Languages. At the present the number of pupils in this Department is small; should an increase require it, additions will be made to the corps of teachers. It is the intention of the Board to continue the exercises of the University through the troubles in which our country is involved, if possible, and to provide ample facilities in the way of teachers and apparatus, for all demands made upon the Institution.
>
> It is said that a few others have been forced to suspend. Let this not be said of Baylor University.[51]

---

[50] R. E. B. Baylor Manuscript.
[51] Baptist State Convention Minutes, 1861, p. 11.

5

The Campuses

ON LOW rolling hills covered with high green grass and dotted with clusters of oak stood "Old Baylor" from 1846 to 1887. Today four columns with a bronze plaque, surrounded by gnarled, moss-covered oaks, and a granite marker on a small rock-strewn hill are all that remain. The columns mark the site of the female department called Academy Hill; the granite slab marks the site of the male department—Allen Hill. On these two hills generations of young ladies and gentlemen trained their minds for the future of their state.

The two hills stand approximately a mile apart, and slope gently toward each other until they reach a small creek called "Jordan" by the students. The buildings on one hill could easily be seen from the other. The town of Independence stood north of Allen Hill in the hollow of both hills.

Academy Hill was the original site of the first building used by the school. This building was a two-story wooden structure erected in the early 1840's and acquired as a part of Independence's bid during the trustees' consideration of a site. When the trustees received the building in 1846 it was in bad shape; there was no flooring between the lower and upper rooms, and the walls were not sealed.[1] New weather board and window lights were needed, and the paint had about all pealed off. By October, the necessary repairs having been made, the building was ready for use.[2]

For the first five years of the school's existence this building was used by both male and female students. In 1851 the male department moved to the stone building on Allen Hill. The old building was left to Clark and the female department. By this time the structure again needed repair; so the trustees au-

[1]Minutes, May 19, 1846, p. 21.
[2]Minutes, Oct. 8, 1846, p. 23.

thorized the building committee to repair the building and make it more comfortable for the female department.[3]

By 1853 the old wooden building was no longer adequate for the needs of the growing department. Increasing demands necessitated the erection of a larger building.[4] Upon the completion of a stone building in 1857, the old building which had been in constant use for eleven years was donated to the contractor of the new building with the stipulation that it be removed within a year.[5]

From the beginning of the school the trustees felt that stone would be the best building material. A quarry was located nearby, which guaranteed a ready supply of building stones. The trustees were fortunate in this, for many of the early colleges of Texas were forced to use wooden structures due to the lack of good stone. Rutersville College, begun by the Methodists in 1840, had only wooden buildings because of the unavailability of stone.[6]

As early as May, 1846, the trustees began to have stone brought to Allen Hill in preparation for the time when a new building could be erected.[7] By 1848 the trustees felt that they could begin construction of a two-story stone building.[8] Actual construction did not begin until 1849, and by the summer of 1850 the building was nearly finished.[9] The stone used in this building as well as future ones was a roughly-hewn hard limestone which, because it sweated, required a covering of plaster.

In the summer of 1851 the furnishings were completed,[10] and on September 1, 1851, Burleson and the male students moved in.[11] The new building on Allen Hill—built at a cost of $6,000—was 36' by 50', with the lower story one large room used as the chapel, and the upper story divided into two classrooms.[12] This edifice was used throughout Baylor's existence at Independence, and the shell stood on the site, long after its abandonment, until 1934.[13]

In 1854 Clark was authorized to raise funds for the build-

---

[3]Minutes, June 18, 1851, p. 51.
[4]Minutes, July 6, 1853, p. 74.
[5]Minutes, Dec. 16, 1857, p. 114.
[6]**Texas Methodist Centennial Yearbook**, p. 45.
[7]Minutes, May 19, 1846, p. 22.
[8]Minutes, June 3, 1848, p. 35.
[9]Minutes, June 15, 1850, p. 48.
[10]Minutes, June 13, 1851, p. 50.
[11]Carroll, **Texas Baptists**, p. 75.
[12]**Ibid.**, p. 234.
[13]Stone marker at the site.

ing of "a commodious stone building upon the present Female Academy lot."[14] By 1855, $5,000 had been raised,[15] and J. Collins was awarded the contract for the building.[16] The trustees adopted Clark's plan for the building,[17] which specified a 40' x 70' two-story stone structure with a portico, cupola and dome.[18]

Construction began in late 1855 or early 1856. When Clark received a $1,000 contribution from Doctor Asa Hoxie, he decided to add another story to the building.[19] By the end of 1857 the exterior was completed, and work on the interior was in the final stages.[20] As early as March 1857 classes were being held in the basement of the building,[21] but full occupance did not occur until 1858. When completed, the building became the pride of the school, and was by far the best of all the buildings built on either hill. The catalogue of 1857 described it as—

> . . . an elegant building, three stories in height, and contains, besides a spacious Audience Hall, a school room, library and apparatus room, and five ample recitation rooms each eighteen by twenty-eight feet. It is handsomely furnished throughout; can be thoroughly ventilated in summer, and comfortably warmed in winter.[22]

A visitor to the campus described the building as "a large and airy building of dressed rock . . . situated upon a beautiful eminence, from which we can view the surrounding country for twenty miles."[23] This building remained in use until the female department's removal to Belton. In 1952 the columns were rebuilt from the ruins to mark the site for future generations.[24]

By 1858 the male department had outgrown its one stone building. The building, completed in 1851, when compared to the female department's elegant new building, was described as "an indifferent old stone building with three or four rooms."[25] Some of the professors were forced to hold their classes in the boarding house.[26] In 1859 the Board decided to work first on

---

[14]Minutes, First Saturday after July 26, 1854, p. 86.
[15]Baptist State Convention Minutes, 1855, p. 23.
[16]Minutes, April 10, 1855, p. 92.
[17]**Ibid.**
[18]Baptist State Convention Minutes, 1855, p. 23.
[19]Carroll, **Texas Baptists,** p. 237.
[20]Minutes, Dec. 15, 1857, p. 112.
[21]Minutes, March 3, 1857, p. 110.
[22]Catalogue, Female Department, 1857, p. 12.
[23]**Texas Baptist Herald,** March 18, 1857.
[24]Bronze plaque on the site.
[25]**Texas Baptist Herald,** March 18, 1857.
[26]**Ibid.**

a "wing building" 36' x 56', and later begin construction of a large main building.[27] In the summer of 1859 Burleson laid the cornerstone of the wing building,[28] and by the time of the Baptist State Convention in 1860 the trustees were able to report that the building was nearly completed, and that work had been begun on the main building which was to be a 101' x 55' three-story structure.[29]

The troubles between Burleson and Clark delayed construction, but after the resignation of the male department the trustees went ahead with their plans.[30] In July, 1861, a portion of the nearly completed wing building collapsed, and the trustees were forced to stop work on the main building and repair the smaller structure.[31] Many people blamed Burleson for the faulty construction, since the building was begun while he was still president. Richard Burleson wrote a letter to the trustees and reminded that his brother had suggested that the walls be plastered inside and out. Instead the trustees had only the front rocks dressed, and the building was painted instead of plastered.[32] The trustees realized their error and accepted the blame for the damage.[33] Although the wing building was finally used, the main building was never completed and remained a shell until torn down in 1934.[34]

A bid submitted to the trustees but not accepted, nevertheless, gives a good description of the type of buildings used by the university. The building proposed was to have an outside dimension of 60' x 94'. The foundation was to be four feet thick and "raised high enough for ventilation under the first floor." In the first story there was to be 10 feet between floor and ceiling with four outside doors and transoms. A hall 10 feet wide would run through the center of the building at right angles. The outside walls were three feet thick and the inside walls had a thickness of two feet. The first floor was divided into eight rooms with 24 windows, eight inside doors, and a fireplace in each room. On the third floor which was to be the

---

[27]Minutes, May 10, 1859, p. 131.

[28]Letter to Brother William from Bud, May 21, 1859 (Baylor at Independence Papers, Texas Collection, Baylor University).

[29]Baptist State Convention Minutes, 1860, p. 13.

[30]Minutes, May 16, 1861, pp. 161-162.

[31]Minutes, July 27, 1861, p. 169.

[32]Letter from Richard Burleson to Hosea Garrett, n.d. (Baylor at Independence Papers, Texas Collection, Baylor University).

[33]Letter from the Board of Trustees to Richard Burleson, July 26, 1861 (Baylor at Independence Papers, Texas Collection, Baylor University).

[34]R. C. Crane, "Tryon Hall," **Baylor Monthly**, V (April, 1929), p. 12.

chapel it was 20 feet from floor to ceiling, and contained 28 windows. There were to be two porticos 12' x 20', each finished with four stone columns rising from the second story. The roof was to be covered with shingles with concealed gutters of tin, and would be painted with "Bridgewater fire proof paint." All of the windows and steps would be cedar with three coats of paint. The building could be completed in 16 months at a cost of $40,977.60.[35]

Other buildings of less durable construction also made up part of the campuses. On the female campus beside the main building stood a large and commodious boarding house. Behind the main building was a garden, the principals house and a dining hall.[36]

On the male campus, situated on the slope a short distance from the stone buildings, stood the octagonal house built by Burleson in 1856.[37] This house served as a boarding house as well as the president's mansion. The large wooden structure was surrounded by a porch on the first and second floors, and was topped by a cupola. Besides the president and his family it could house about twenty boarders. A visitor to the newly constructed house gave this description: "We paid a visit to his new dwelling, and through the many windings, climbing up we at length reached the apex of the octagon." The visitor described the beautiful view of the plain and valley "laden with live-oaks and evergreens."[38]

Besides the octagon house there were at least two small dormitories. These were "one story frame houses neatly made, with two rooms and stack chimneys."[39]

The grounds of both campuses were enclosed with a fence and contained a well,[40] as well as benches and tables. Also in shady out-of-the-way spots were located those structures necessitated by the lack of plumbing. In 1855 the building committee of the Board of Trustees was requested to build suitable privies for both departments,[41] but feeling the task a bit beneath their dignity, they turned the responsibility over to Burleson

---

[35]Letter from John S. Miner to the Building Committee, March 29, 1859 (Baylor at Independence Papers, Texas Collection, Baylor University).

[36]Model (Texas Collection, Baylor University).

[37]Letter from R. C. Burleson to Richard Burleson, Sept. 16, 1856 (R. C. Burleson Papers, Texas Collection, Baylor University).

[38]**Texas Baptist Herald**, March 18, 1857.

[39]Minutes, July 30, 1852, p. 70.

[40]Minutes, March 5, 1856, p. 103.

[41]Minutes, April 10, 1855, p. 93.

and Clark.[42] Although there is no evidence as to what Clark and Burleson felt about this responsibility, it would be logical to surmise that the needed structures were built.

Independence today is a small, quiet village nestled among rolling green hills. About the town one can see houses built when "Old Baylor" was thriving, but on the two hills—except for four columns, a granite marker, and a few scattered building stones—nothing remains of the historic old halls which once reverberated with the voices of Burleson, Clark, and a host of eager and not-so-eager scholars.

---

[42]Minutes, June 19, 1855, p. 94.

6

Curriculum and Student Life

THE DIFFERENCES between the Baylor student of today and yesterday are in many ways superficial. Remove the automobile, television, movies and Hi Fi, and today's student would be basically the same as the student of "Old Baylor."

Most of the students enrolled in the university were in the preparatory with the enrollment of the collegiate department relatively small. A two-year course of study in the preparatory department was necessary before most students could enter the collegiate department. The course of study in the preparatory department included English grammar, arithmetic, Latin, geography, penmanship, Greek grammar, American history, bookkeeping, and readings in Caesar and Virgil.[1]

A young man who satisfactorily completed the requirements in the preparatory department could then begin work in the collegiate department. Several choices were open to such a young man; he could take a course of study leading to an A.B. degree, or he could take a three-year scientific course. The law school was another possibility, or the young man could do work in preparation for the ministry.

The A.B. required four years of study. A freshman was required to do satisfactory work in algebra, plane geometry, Latin grammar, Greek grammar, and readings in Sallust, Xenophon, Cicero, Homer, and the Greek New Testament. In the sophomore year further studies in Homer and in geometry were required. The sophomore also took ancient history, plane and spherical trigonometry, natural philosophy, natural history, and readings in Thucydides and Horace. During the third year the student took courses in surveying and navigation, Spanish or French, German, Greek and Roman history, analytical geometry, and chemistry, with readings in Demosthenes, Tacitus,

[1]Catalogue, 1851-1852, p. 7.

Aeschylas, and Euripides. The senior completed his studies with astronomy, intellectual philosophy, English history and literature, German, Spanish or French, the United States Constitution, moral science, political economy, geology, differential and integral calculus, elements of criticism, and evidences of Christianity.[2]

The three-year scientific course included studies in several areas of mathematics—algebra, geometry, calculus, and mensuration (finding lengths, areas, and volumes). Other science courses such as geology, chemistry, hydrostatics and hydraulics, anatomy, hygiene, mineralogy, botany, and astronomy were part of the required subjects. Besides the science and mathematics courses the science student took modern and ancient history, logic, evidences of Christianity, political economy, rhetoric, moral philosophy, and analogy of religion and nature.[3]

The ministerial student took the regular A.B. courses but could study Hebrew instead of the required modern languages.[4]

In all departments special attention was given to physical fitness, which was considered necessary for preserving health and thereby obtaining the highest value of education.[5]

The preparatory school in the female department required a course of study similar to the male department. The course of study for an A.B. was as follows:

Freshman Year—arithmetic, mental philosophy, grammar, Watt's *On the Mind,* English composition, first Latin book, French reader.

Sophomore Year—algebra, natural philosophy, chemistry, Latin grammar and reader, French, anatomy, and physiology.

Junior Year—geometry, meterology, logic, Virgil, French, astronomy, and rhetoric.

Senior Year—trigonometry and mensuration, elements of criticism, intellectual philosophy, evidences of Christianity, and *Cornelius Nepas.* Throughout the course the girls had instruction in composition, elocution, and vocal music.[6] To further develop her as a cultured and gracious lady the young student could take courses in drawing, painting, and embroidery.[7]

Both male and female collegiate students had four one-hour

---

[2]Catalogue, Male Department, 1857, pp. 11-12.
[3]**Ibid.,** p. 14.
[4]**Ibid.,** p. 13.
[5]Catalogue, Male Department, 1855, n.p.
[6]Catalogue, Female Department, 1857, pp. 21-22.
[7]**Ibid.,** p. 11.

classes a day. The first fifteen minutes of each class were used in reviewing the previous day's work,[8] and compositions were required semi-monthly.[9] The daily schedule was so arranged as to give the students ten minutes of "recreation" between classes.[10]

Immediately after each class the professor affixed a numerical grade after each students name. For a perfect recitation the grade was ten. If a student was not prepared he was given a zero. If the student had a satisfactory excuse the zero still stood, but if there was no excuse, he got the zero and demerits as well.[11]

Before students were admitted to the university they were required to read the laws of the university and sign a declaration of their intentions to obey them.[12] These laws were designed so that the institution would be conducted by "principles of elevated morality."[13] According to these regulations no profane language was allowed on campus, the boys could not carry or possess pistols, knives, or any other weapons; there was to be no gambling or visiting of "dramshops" and "drinking houses;" and the student was not to be out of his room after 9:00 p.m. or to "engage in any nocturnal disorder or revelings." The student was expected to "pursue diligently the course of study prescribed by the faculty," and could not leave the school without the permission of the faculty.[14]

A system of demerits was used for disciplinary purposes. Disturbances on the part of a student in the chapel, lecture room, or any part of the campus incurred from one to ten demerits. If a student was not present at roll call, and had no acceptable excuse, he received from one to ten demerits. A student absent from his room after dark and before 9:00 p.m. was given five demerits; if he came in after 9:00 p.m. he was given ten demerits. Whenever a student accumulated thirty demerits his parents were informed; if a student's demerits totaled one hundred, he was dismissed from the school.[15]

The girls had to observe similar rules in their deportment, and even their apparel was regulated—the young girls were to

[8]Catalogue, Male Department, 1855, n.p.
[9]Catalogue, 1851, p. 11.
[10]Catalogue, Male Department, 1854, p. 4.
[11]Catalogue, Male Department, 1855, n.p.
[12]**Laws of Baylor University**, 1859, p. 6.
[13]Minutes, Dec. 17, 1853, p. 79.
[14]**Ibid.**, pp. 78-79.
[15]Catalogue, Male Department, 1855, n.p.

wear "bonnets of white straw, plainly trimmed with pink ribbon of solid color (may be lined with pink); no flounces or tucks. Gay and expensive ribbons were not allowed nor were extreme fashions indulged. Jewelry, with the exception of a plain breast-pin, was prohibited. No girl was permitted to appear in public unless dressed according to regulations.[16] These rules may have pleased the parents, but the girls probably had other thoughts about them.

The girls as well as the boys were required to attend daily opening exercises in which a passage of scripture was read, prayer was offered, and hymns were sung. The young ladies who boarded at the school were required to attend the Sunday School of their choice.[17] As is still true today the girls of "Old Baylor" were kept under stricter observance than were the boys. All young ladies from out of town were expected to board at the school. The girls had stated hours for study and recreation; they could attend parties and have visitors only at the discretion of the principal. Under no circumstances were they allowed to be away from the school at night.[18]

Students of the Independence period wrote letters home much like today, and if the dates were not given, very few differences would be noticed:

> I am doing very well in my studies and I am not studying too hard either—sometimes I feel like chiding myself for studying as little as I do. He (father) repeated his advice to me about Economy—I am glad he does so—though I believe I have less disposition to spend foolishly than he thinks. . . .[19]

One young scholar proudly informed his father of his progress:

> I am well satisfied here. I am learning faster than I ever learnt (*sic*) in my life. My teachers returns (*sic*) their respects to you. We have excellant (*sic*) Teachers here they take all of the pains with the students that is (*sic*) necessary to advance them.[20]

[16]Catalogue, Female Department, 1857, p. 17.
[17]**Ibid.**, p. 14.
[18]**Ibid.**, p. 18.
[19]Letter from M. M. Vanderhurst to his brother, Dr. W. D. Eastland, May 17, 1859 (Baylor at Independence Papers, Texas Collection, Baylor University).
[20]Letter from Johnathan A. McGary Jr. to Johnathan A. McGary Sr., Oct. 31, 1859 (Baylor at Independence Papers, Texas Collection, Baylor University).

After receiving such a letter the father may have had some doubts as to the academic progress of his son.

In another letter a son wrote his father requesting that he send socks, candles, and "$3 for some debts."[21]

The desire to go home during vacations was as strong then as now. One boy informed his older brother that parents of many of the boys were sending them horses to ride home. He pleads with his brother to send even the little white mule as that would be better than walking.[22]

Although studies and letter writing consumed most of the student's time, there were other activities which helped while away the free hours. The girls would occasionally go "dewberrying" or picnicking not too far from the campus, and there was an occasional party. On special days—such as San Jacinto Day—there would be a speech from such a notable as Sam Houston. There were also picnics and other festivities.[23] Commencement was a time of speeches and parties,[24] concerts and picnics. From time to time the female department held concerts,[25] and the boys had debates. Debating was a favorite pastime, with the boys engaged in heated and exciting controversies as indicated in a letter from H. B. Carroll:

> Our debates go on gloriously. I'm continually tossed about on the waves of exciting controversy. . . . I warent (*sic*) you we often cross swords over historical queries and technicalities. The old Charles the First question comes up next Saturday and I as usual will oppose his execution.[26]

Several societies were organized by the male students: the Philomathesian Society, organized in 1851;[27] the Erisophians, organized in 1853;[28] and the Adelphian Society, organized in 1854.[29] These societies held weekly meetings for debates, lectures, and readings of essays.[30] The "Philos" and the "Sophies"

---

[21]Letter from J. T. Good to his father, May 8, 1865 (Baylor at Independence Papers, Texas Collection, Baylor University).

[21]Letter from J. T. Good to his father, May 8, 1865 (Baylor at Independence Papers, Texas Collection, Baylor University).

[22]Letter from M. M. Vanderhurst to Dr. W. D. Eastland, May 17, 1859.

[23]Letter from Florence Davis to her father, April 29, 1859 (Baylor at Independence Papers, Texas Collection, Baylor University).

[24]Printed invitation, Friday evening, June 22, 1860 (Baylor at Independence Papers, Texas Collection, Baylor University).

[25]Minutes, June 30, 1859, p. 133.

[26]Letter from H. B. Carroll to Colonel J. C. Barrow, Oct. 30, 1859 (Baylor at Independence Papers, Texas Collection, Baylor University).

[27]Catalogue, Male Department, 1854, p. 8.

[30]**Ibid.**

edited papers and maintained a reading room which contained a very large and well-filled library.[31] Other societies and clubs such as the Historo-Biographical Society,[32] and the Wheeler Law Club[33] were organized, but they did not last.

Revivals played an important part in the life of the institution. Although Baylor was a Baptist school, many of the students were not professing Christians; in 1855 only 24 of the 102 male students were church members.[34] There were never more than eight ministerial students attending Baylor at one time.[35] With so many non-Christian students there was a need for periodical revivals. The Board of Trustees disclaimed any right to compel pupils to attend religious meetings, but felt it for the best interests of the pupils that Clark and Burleson cooperate with the pastor of the Independence Baptist Church in all revivals and encourage attendance of all the pupils unless against the known wishes of the parents.[36] In one revival five young men professed Christ and were received for baptism. One of the five was the last of the senior class who had not professed religion.[37] During the many revivals a large number of students joined the church.[38] Baylor then, as now, was concerned not only with the academic welfare of its students, but with their spiritual condition as well.

Some of the boys then as now were not content with the duties of study, or with picnics and the like; they preferred to create their own amusements; so from time to time students were brought before the trustees to account for their misdeeds. For example, two students were brought before the Board because they "got drunk . . . and interrupted the exhibition of the female department."[39] One young man was charged with "idleness and failure to study," being absent from class several times, having no acceptable excuse, and heading a crowd of boys in an assault on the post office.[40] Another student was charged with habitual neglect of studies, use of profane language in the presence of Professor Fitzgerald, being in company

---

[31]Letter from H. B. Carroll to Colonel J. C. Barrow, Oct. 30, 1859.
[32]**Ibid.**
[33]Catalogue, Male Department, 1857, p. 25.
[34]Baptist State Convention Minutes, p. 22.
[35]Baptist State Convention Minutes, 1859, p. 10.
[36]Minutes, Dec. 18, 1857, p. 116.
[37]**Texas Baptist,** Sept. 26, 1855.
[38]Baptist State Convention Minutes, 1855, p. 22.
[39]Minutes, Dec. 3, 1858, p. 123.
[40]Handwritten paper (Baylor at Independence Papers, Texas Collection, Baylor University).

with "midnight revellers," and intoxication.[41] Students such as these were usually expelled, but were allowed to re-enter at the next session if they promised better conduct.[42]

Examinations and commencement were the highlights of the year with the students and faculty doing all they could to make the event memorable.

Examinations were conducted by a visiting examining committee, and the students were tested over "the most intricate sentences and idiomatic phrases in the Latin, Greek, French, German, and Spanish languages, the most obtruse and knotty problems in mathematics, from algebra to Integral Calculus, the most profound and redondite principles in natural, intellectual, and moral philosophy . . ." The girls were examined for proficiency in arithmetic, and higher mathematics, English composition, history, rhetoric, botany, Latin, French, and moral and intellectual philosophy.[43] As a part of the examinations the students delivered speeches, addresses and essays.[44]

The examinations of 1855 lasted four days. Each night there were speeches by the gentlemen or compositions by the ladies all interspersed with music. On the last day Burleson delivered his literary address before the Philomathesian and Erisophian Societies.[45] The program for one such night was as follows:

Prayer
Music
1. Footprints of Man, Charles R. Breedlove, Independence.
2. Destiny of Man, Taylor M. Cox, Huntsville.

Music

3. A Resolute Mind Is Omnipotent, Blackstone H. Davis, Austin
4. Eulogy on General Green, H. C. Oliphant, Huntsville.

Music

5. Stability of the Union, Daniel Bradshaw, Preston.
6. Americans Kneel to None but God, Thomas J. Goree, Madisonville.

Music

7. The Indian Race, William H. Jones, Bastrop.
8. The Chief Glory of the Nation, Daniel E. Thomson, Nashville.

Music

---

[41]Minutes, Dec. 18, 1853, p. 81.
[42]**Ibid.**, p. 82.
[43]**Texas Baptist**, July 26, 1860.
[44]**Texas Baptist**, Jan. 13, 1858.
[45]**Washington American** (Washington, Texas) Dec. 14, 1855.

Debate on the utility of studying the ancient languages. Charles T. Kavanaugh—Chappell Hill and W. H. Parks—Anderson.[46]

The speeches at these programs were lengthy and filled with the excessive verbiage popular in those days. One such speech entitled "Christopher Columbus" began—

> Many years ago long before the mighty forests which over enveloped this fair land had resounded the echo of the woodmans' axe, lived a youth in that fair and classic land far beyond the Atlantic whose very name is the embodiment of music, poetry and love.[47]

The commencement exercise was the culminating exercise and lasted most of the day. The printed program of one of the female commencements gives a good picture of what these exercises were like: At 11 a.m. the annual literary address was delivered by William Montgomery, Esquire on the subject, "The Mission of Educated Woman in America." At 2 p.m. the program resumed with a prayer followed by a number of essays interspersed with music:

Essay — Miss Mary Allcorn—"Is Genius Compatible with Domestic Felicity?"
Essay — Miss Emeline Allcorn—"The Interest Attached to the Tombs of Poets and Other Distinguished Persons."
Music — Vocal Duet.
Essay — Miss Sarah F. Chambers—"Human Pursuits."
Essay — Miss Mary A. Eddins—"The Conqueror's Trophies."
Music — Instrumental Duet.
Essay — Miss Catherine Clark—"The Brevity of Life."
Essay — Miss Rebecca Skelton—"The Hill of Science."
Music — Instrumental.
Essay — Miss Rachael Barry—"The Mission of Beauty."
Essay — Miss Sallie McNiel—"Foot Prints on the Sands of Time."
Music — Vocal Duet.
Essay — Miss Bettie B. Carter—"Natural Provisions for Human Happiness."
Essay — Miss Mary McKellar—"Self Culture"
Music — Instrumental.
Essay — Miss Dora Pettus—"The Religion of Nature."

---

[46]Printed program (Baylor at Independence Papers, Texas Collection, Baylor University).

[47]Speech of Johnathan A. McGary Jr. (Baylor at Independence Papers, Texas Collection, Baylor University).

Essay — Miss Julia A. Robertson—"The Trans Atlantic Telegraph."
Music — Song.
Essay — Miss Mary T. Whitesides—"The Mission of Liberty."
Essay — Miss Fannie A. Rogers—"The Responsibilities of Genius."
Valedictory — Miss T. A. Rogers.
Baccalaureate Address.
Conferring of the Diplomas.[48]

As part of the commencement program medals were awarded to students deserving special recognition. A medal was awarded for the best specimen of penmanship, for the best translation into Latin of a portion of Macaulay's *History of England,* for the best original oration, and for the highest number of merit marks in mathematics.[49]

The certificates or diplomas awarded specified the branches in which each student had a full and correct knowledge,[50] and cost the graduates ten dollars.[51] With this final act in the academic career of the young scholars, they were now fully prepared to go out and become the doctors, lawyers, teachers, pastors, homemakers, and fathers and mothers of future generations of Texans. From the first graduating class to the last at Independence, Baylor graduates contributed greatly to the progress and greatness of their state, and became distinguished and honored citizens of Texas.

[48]**Texas Baptist**, Dec. 9, 1858.
[49]Catalogue, Male Department, 1855, n.p.
[50]Minutes, Dec. 21, 1854, pp. 89-90.
[51]Minutes, Dec. 18, 1856, p. 108.
[52]Ray, **Austin Colony Pioneers**, p. 42.

Conclusion

With high academic and moral standards, Baylor University stood for quality rather than quantity:

> This shows more solicitude to make scholars than to number graduates. A large number of graduates is not honorable to an institution of learning. The best schools with even very large attendance, have but few full graduates . . . large classes would show defective work and graduation by favor rather than on merit and scholarship. Where a high standard is maintained, comparatively few reach it. The less number of graduates in proportion to attendance, the more value may be attached to a diploma and to the instruction and college training afforded.[52]

With the move of Burleson and his faculty to Waco, only one phase of Baylor's long history had passed. The then young institution would pass through many more trials and tribulations, but always the determination of the trustees, teachers, and students was sufficient to keep the institution going. The school would continue in Independence until its removal to Waco in spite of difficult problems which had been the downfall of so many other institutions. Always in the minds of the trustees were the words of those beleaguered trustees in 1861—". . . a few others have been forced to suspend. Let this not be said of Baylor University."

Appendixes

APPENDIX I

TRUSTEES OF BAYLOR UNIVERSITY 1845-1861

1845 - 1846
R. E. Baylor—President
E. W. Taylor—Secretary
J. G. Thomas
James S. Lester
R. B. Jarman
Nelson Kavanaugh
Oran Drake
James L. Farquhar
A. G. Haynes
William M. Tryon
James Huckins
Eli Mercer
Aaron Shannon
Robert S. Armstead

1846 - 1847
William Tryon—President
E. W. Taylor—Secretary
J. G. Thomas
James S. Lester
Nelson Kavanaugh
James L. Farquhar
A. G. Haynes
Aaron Shannon
R. E. B. Baylor
R. B. Jarman
James Huckins
Robert Armstead
Eli Mercer

1847 - 1848
William Tryon—President
E. W. Taylor—Secretary
R. E. B. Baylor
James S. Lester
J. G. Thomas
Nelson Kavanaugh
James L. Farquhar
Oran Drake
A. G. Haynes
Aaron Shannon
James Huckins
Robert Armstead (resigned)
Eli Mercer
R. B. Jarman

1848 - 1849
Hosea Garrett—President
J. G. Thomas—Secretary
A. G. Haynes, Treasurer
R. E. B. Baylor
James S. Lester
James Huckins
R. B. Jarman
Nelson Kavanaugh
James L. Farquhar
Aaron Shannon
Oran Drake
Eli Mercer
E. W. Taylor
Terrell J. Jackson

1849 - 1850
Hosea Garrett—President
J. G. Thomas—Clerk
A. G. Haynes, Treasurer
R. E. B. Baylor
James S. Lester
R. B. Jarmin
Nelson Kavanaugh
James L. Farquhar

Aaron Shannon
J. W. D. Creath
James R. Hinds
Terrell J. Jackson
A. S. Lipscomb
Oran Drake (resigned)

1850 - 1851

Hosea Garrett—President
J. G. Thomas—Secretary
A. G. Haynes—Treasurer
R. E. B. Baylor
James S. Lester
R. B. Jarman
Nelson Kavanaugh
James L. Farquhar
Aaron Shannon
J. W. D. Creath
James R. Hinds
Terrell J. Jackson
A. S. Lipscomb
George W. Baines

1851 - 1852

Hosea Garrett—President
Nelson Kavanaugh—Secretary
A. G. Haynes—Treasurer
R. E. B. Baylor
A. S. Lipscomb
A. C. Horton
J. W. D. Creath
George W. Baines
J. G. Thomas
James L. Farquhar
Aaron Shannon
James S. Lester
Terrell J. Jackson
J. W. Barnes
R. B. Jarman

1852 - 1853

Hosea Garrett—President
Nelson Kavanaugh—Secretary
A. G. Haynes—Treasurer
R. E. B. Baylor
A. S. Lipscomb
A. C. Horton
J. W. D. Creath
George W. Baines
J. G. Thomas
James L. Farquhar
Aaron Shannon
R. B. Jarman
J. S. Lester
T. J. Jackson
J. W. Barnes

1853 - 1854

Hosea Garrett—President
Nelson Kavanaugh—Secretary
A. G. Haynes—Treasurer
R. E. B. Baylor
A. S. Lipscomb
A. C. Horton
J. W. D. Creath
George W. Baines
J. G. Thomas
James L. Farquhar
Aaron Shannon
R. B. Jarman
J. S. Lester
Terrell J. Jackson
J. W. Barnes

1854 - 1855

Hosea Garrett—President
Nelson Kavanaugh—Secretary
A. G. Haynes—Treasurer
R. E. B. Baylor
A. S. Lipscomb (died)
A. C. Horton
J. W. D. Creath
George W. Baines
J. G. Thomas
James L. Farquhar
Aaron Shannon
R. B. Jarman
J. S. Lester
Terrell J. Jackson
J. W. Barnes

1855 - 1856

Hosea Garrett—President
Nelson Kavanaugh—Secretary
A. G. Haynes—Treasurer
R. E. B. Baylor
G. W. Graves
A. C. Horton

J. W. D. Creath
George W. Baines
J. G. Thomas
James L. Farquhar
Aaron Shannon
R. B. Jarman
J. S. Lester
Terrell J. Jackson
J. W. Barnes

1856 - 1857
Hosea Garrett—President
Nelson Kavanaugh—Secretary
A. G. Haynes—Treasurer
R. E. B. Baylor
G. W. Graves
A. C. Horton
J. W. D. Creath
George W. Baines
J. G. Thomas
James L. Farquhar
Aaron Shannon
R. B. Jarman
J. S. Lester
Terrell J. Jackson
J. W. Barnes

1857 - 1858
Hosea Garrett—President
Nelson Kavanaugh—Secretary
A. G. Haynes—Treasurer
R. E. B. Baylor
G. W. Graves
A. C. Horton
J. W. D. Creath
George W. Baines
J. G. Thomas
James L. Farquhar
Aaron Shannon
R. B. Jarman
J. S. Lester
Terrell J. Jackson
J. W. Barnes

1858 - 1859
Hosea Garrett—President
Nelson Kavanaugh—Secretary
A. G. Haynes—Treasurer
R. E. B. Baylor
G. W. Graves
A. C. Horton
J. W. D. Creath
George W. Baines (resigned)
J. G. Thomas
James L. Farquhar
Aaron Shannon
R. B. Jarman
J. S. Lester
Terrell J. Jackson
J. W. Barnes

1859 - 1860
Hosea Garrett—President
Nelson Kavanaugh—Secretary
A. G. Haynes—Treasurer
R. E. B. Baylor
G. W. Graves
A. C. Horton
J. W. D. Creath
E. G. Mays
J. G. Thomas
James L. Farquhar
Aaron Shannon
R. B. Jarman
J. S. Lester
Terrell J. Jackson
J. W. Barnes

1860 - 1861
Hosea Garrett—President
Nelson Kavanaugh—Secretary
A. G. Haynes—Treasurer
R. E. B. Baylor
G. W. Graves
A. C. Horton
J. W. D. Creath
E. G. Mays
J. G. Thomas
James L. Farquhar
Aaron Shannon
R. B. Jarman
J. S. Lester
Terrell J. Jackson
J. W. Barnes

APPENDIX II

Faculties

1846 - 1847

Henry F. Gillett—Preparatory Department

1847 - 1848

Henry L. Graves—President
Henry F. Gillett—Preparatory Department

1848 - 1849

Henry L. Graves—President
Henry F. Gillett—Preparatory Department
Daniel Witt—Spanish and Ancient Languages
Warren Conley—Tutor
J. H. Finch—Tutor

1849 - 1850

Henry L. Graves—President
Daniel Witt—Spanish and Ancient Languages

1850 - 1851

Henry L. Graves—President
Augustus Guttlar—French and German
Mrs. Louisa Guttlar—Music and Fancy Work

1851 - 1852 — Male Department

R. C. Burleson—President, Ancient Languages, Intellectual Philosophy and Belles Lettres
S. G. O'Bryan—Mathematics and Moral Philosophy
B. S. Fitzgerald—Ancient Languages, Principal of the Preparatory Department
W. L. Foster—French, Spanish, Mathematics
Thomas G. Edwards—English Literature, Tutor in the Preparatory Department

1851 - 1852 — Female Department

Horace Clark—Principal, Ancient Languages, Moral and Intellectual Philosophy
Miss Harriet L. Davis—Mathematics, Natural Science, French, Drawing, Painting, Embroidery
Mrs. Martha D. Clark—History, English Literature
Miss E. B. Scott—Music

1852 - 1853 — Male Department

R. C. Burleson—President, Ancient Languages, Intellectual Philosophy, Belles Lettres, Spanish
J. B. Stiteler—Natural Sciences—German
S. G. O'Bryan—Mathematics, French
B. S. Fitzgerald—Ancient Languages, Principal of the Preparatory Department

1852 - 1853 — Female Department
Horace Clark—Principal, Ancient Languages, Intellectual Philosophy
Mrs. Martha D. Clark—History, English Literature
Miss Harriet L. Davis—Mathematics, Natural Sciences, French, Drawing, Painting, Embroidery

1853 - 1854 — Male Department
R. C. Burleson—President, Ancient Languages, Intellectual Philosophy, Belles Lettres, Spanish
J. B. Stiteler—Natural Sciences, German
S. G. O'Bryan—Mathematics, French
B. S. Fitzgerald—Ancient Languages, Principal of the Preparatory Department

1853 - 1854 — Female Department
Horace Clark—Principal, Ancient Languages, Intellectual Philosophy
Mrs. Martha D. Clark—History, English Literature
Miss Harriet L. Davis—Mathematics, Natural Sciences, French, Drawing, Painting, Embroidery

1854 - 1855 — Male Department
R. C. Burleson—President, Latin, Greek, Spanish, Belles Lettres
J. B. Stiteler—Natural Sciences, German
James A. Johnson—Mathematics
B. S. Fitzgerald—Ancient Languages, Principal of the Preparatory Department
James L. Smith—Teacher in the Preparatory Department

1854 - 1855 — Female Department
Horace Clark—Principal, Ancient Languages, Intellectual Philosophy
Mrs. Martha D. Clark—History, English Literature
Miss Harriet L. Davis—Mathematics, Natural Sciences, French, Drawing, Painting, Embroidery

1855 - 1856 — Male Department
R. C. Burleson—President, Latin, Greek, Spanish, Belles Lettres
J. B. Stiteler—Moral, Mental and Natural Sciences, German
Gilbert L. Morgan—Mathematics
Stephen D. Rowe—Ancient Languages
James L. Smith—Principal of the Preparatory Department

1855 - 1856 — Female Department

Horace Clark—Principal, Ancient Languages, Intellectual Philosophy
Mrs. Martha D. Clark—History, English Literature
Miss Harriet L. Davis—Mathematics, Natural Sciences, French, Drawing, Painting, Embroidery

1856 - 1857 — Male Department

R. C. Burleson—President, Latin, Greek, Spanish, Belles Lettres
J. B. Stiteler—Moral, Mental, and Natural Sciences, German
Gilbert L. Morgan—Mathematics
Stephen D. Rowe—Ancient Languages
James L. Smith—Principal of the Preparatory Department

1856 - 1857 — Female Department

Horace Clark—Principal, Ancient Languages, Intellectual Philosophy
Mary R. Davis—History, Rhetoric, English Literature
Mary R. Graves—Mathematics, Natural Science
Agnes Steinhaur—French, German, Drawing, Painting

1857 - 1858 — Male Department

R. C. Burleson—President, Latin, Greek, Spanish
David R. Wallace—Natural Science, French
Richard B. Burleson—Moral and Mental Philosophy, Political Economy, Belles Lettres
O. H. Leland—Mathematics, Astronomy
Charles T. Kavanaugh—Ancient Languages, Tutor in the Preparatory Department
James L. Smith—Principal of the Preparatory Department
F. Keifer—German

Law Department

R. T. Wheeler
R. E. B. Baylor
W. P. Rogers

1857 - 1858 — Female Department

Horace Clark—Principal, Ancient Languages, Moral and Intellectual Philosophy
Miss Mary R. Davis—Rhetoric, Belles Lettres
Louis Franke—Guitar, Vocal Music, Piano Forte, German
Mrs. Martha D. Clark—Teacher in the Preparatory Department
Miss Raiford A. Smith—Assistant Teacher of Music

1858 - 1859 — Male Department

R. C. Burleson—President, Moral Philosophy, Spanish, Belles Lettres
Richard B. Burleson—Vice-President, Natural Science
David R. Wallace—Latin, Greek, French

Oscar H. Leland—Mathematics, Mechanical Philosophy, Astronomy
Louis Franke—German
James L. Smith—Principal of the Preparatory Department
William H. Long—Tutor

Law Department

R. E. B. Baylor
W. P. Rogers
John Sayles

1858 - 1859 — Female Department

Horace Clark—Principal, Moral and Intellectual Philosophy
B. S. Fitzgerald—Ancient Languages, Mathematics
Mary R. Davis—English Language and Literature
Miss Liane De Lassaulx—Modern Languages, Embroidery
Mrs. Sarah J. Scott—Preparatory Department
D. W. Chase—Principal of the Music Department, Vocal and Instrumental Music
Miss Mary D. Chase—Harp, Piano, Vocal Music
Miss Carrie L. Chase—Drawing, Painting, Wax Work
Oscar A. Chase—Piano and Guitar
W. Willeric—Superintendent of the Gymnasium

1859 - 1860 — Male Department

R. C. Burleson—President, Moral Philosophy, Belles Lettres, Spanish
Richard B. Burleson—Vice-President, Natural Science, Librarian
David R. Wallace—Latin, Greek, French
Oscar H. Leland—Mathematics, Mechanical Philosophy, Astronomy
Louis Franke—German
William H. Lang—Tutor

1859 - 1860 — Female Department

Horace Clark—Principal, Moral and Intellectual Philosophy
B. S. Fitzgerald—Ancient Languages, Mathematics
Mrs. Liane Willeric—Modern Language, Embroidery
Mrs. Sarah Scott—Preparatory Department
D. W. Chase—Vocal and Instrumental Music
Miss Carrie L. Chase—Drawing, Painting, Wax Work
Miss Mary D. Chase—Harp, Piano, Vocal Music
Oscar A. Chase—Piano and Guitar

1860 - 1861 — Male Department

R. C. Burleson—President, Moral Philosophy, Belles Lettres, Spanish
Richard B. Burleson—Vice-President, Natural Sciences, Librarian
David R. Wallace—Latin, Greek, French
Oscar H. Leland—Mathematics, Mechanical Philosophy, Astronomy
George W. Willeric—Modern Languages

1860 - 1861 — Female Department

Horace Clark—Principal, Moral and Intellectual Philosophy
B. S. Fitzgerald—Ancient Languages, Mathematics
Mrs. Liane Willeric—Modern Languages, Embroidery
Mrs. Sarah Scott—Preparatory Department
D. W. Chase—Vocal and Instrumental Music
Miss Carrie L. Chase—Drawing, Painting, Wax Work
Miss Mary D. Chase—Harp, Piano, Vocal Music
Oscar A. Chase—Piano, Guitar

Graduates

Male Department

1854
Stephen Decatur Rowe

1856
Madison Milton Callaway
Thomas Jefferson Goree
Charles Thomas Kavanaugh
Oscar Hopestill Leland
William Henry Parks
Curtis Hudson Oliphant

1857
William Baldwin Denson
George Eaves Davis
Cicero Jenkins
Joseph Peter Jackson
John Franklin Smith

1858
James Thomas Daniel
Charles Richard Breedlove
James Brooke Thomas

1859
James Marshall Arnold
Daniel Abner Bradshaw
Lucius Henry Brown
George Lewis Chandler
Joseph Emory Deupree
William Henry Long
Wythe Walker Wheeler

1860
Timothy T. Dunklin
Pincknie Harris
Thomas J. Cleaveland
Benjamin H. Thompson
James A. Dickie

Female Department

1855
Mary G. Kavanaugh

1856
Zilphia G. Fuller
Carrie Mooney

1857
Ophelia V. Jenkins

1858
Emeline Allcorn
Mary Allcorn
Rachael Barry
Bettie B. Carter
Sarah H. Chambers
Catharine Clark
Mary A. Eddins
Sarah J. McNiel
Mary S. McKellar
Dora A. Pettus
Mary T. Whiteside
Julia A. Robertson
Rebecca S. Skelton
Fannie A. Rogers

1859
Lucy A. Atkinson

1860
Adelia H. Jarman
Gertrude Hogue
Sarah Posey Traynham

APPENDIX IV

Scott Letters

Mrs. Sarah Jane Scott was a teacher in the female department preparatory school. She began teaching at the school during the 1858-1859 school year and continued through 1861. Some of her letters to her brother George Duff have been recently discovered which reveal some new insights into the life of a teacher of that day. Life for the school teacher was filled with long hours of difficult labors: in a letter to her brother Mrs. Scott describes her routine:

> Do you wish to know how I am doing these days? Imagine yourself at the school room door, and recall that little scene. I am just as busy as you found me that day for six hours every day, which is better than it used to be for I used to teach seven. There is more to do in my department but I have assistance. There are now fifty-three girls in my department, and I think I have good reason to suppose that my own popularity as a teacher, has caused that department to improve so rapidly.[1]

Mrs. Scott, in spite of the long hours of labor, seemed to be satisfied with her job, but still she was homesick:

> I am very well satisfied with my position, altho' I teach the children, I believe I am looked upon with a great deal of respect in this community, you know I have always been where ever I have taught. . . . I am very cheerful and well satisfied generally, but there are times when I feel the want of home and its dear ties, my business is interesting, my pleasures are intellectual, but these do not always satisfy . . .[2]

However, in April of 1860, Mrs. Scott painted a different picture of her life at the school:

> . . . altho' I am sorry to have to say so, if I keep on as I have to do in . . . this establishment, I shall give out, and as I may not die immediately, I shall be on somebody's hands,

[1]Letter from Mrs. Sarah Jane Scott to her brother, George Duff, January 24, 1860.

[2]**Ibid.**

> and I don't know whom to turn to, . . . I have been thinking for some time on the subject, and it seems to me that it would be better for me to change my situation than to wear out as I must do here. No teacher in the school except the music teachers has as much to do as I have.[3]

Mrs. Scott then relates to her brother the reasons for her discontent—

> I govern a room of sixty-five girls and children, and hear lessons six hours a day, and am in the room to open and close school besides. And last week Mr. Clark very cooly made the arrangement for me to add another hour, altho' our agreement the first of this term was for six hours, that is I was to have an easier time and take the same salary but he does not remember *that* I suppose, and besides for all of the time I have taught I have received only one hundred & eighty five dollars with which I paid debts . . .[4]

Her letter reveals the financial difficulties that were plaguing the school and how Clark was trying to somehow make ends meet:

> . . . and when I offered last week to give them (her creditors) an order on Mr. Clark they refused to take it. Now if he did this way about paying his teachers & was very kind & considerate one might go on with him & wait, but when he seems perfectly regardless of you in every way it is not very agreeable—the first of the term or soon after—I wrote him a note explaining that I wanted my money to pay my debts if he could pay me without too much inconvenience but—considerately added that if he had more demands than he could meet I would wait. He did not take the slightest note of my request or forbearance, and that is his way of doing, but if he was the most agreeable man in the world, if I was getting a large salary I should wear out here, . . .[5]

Mrs. Scott then reveals to her brother some of the other duties required of her:

> . . . where I have duties out of school as well as in and have to room with fourteen girls. If I could have the chance to take a little nap during the noontime it would help me a great deal, but there is never for me one moment of quiet

[3]Letter from Mrs. Sarah Jane Scott to her brother, George Duff, April 12, 1860.
[4]**Ibid.**
[5]**Ibid.**

> and rest, except for after the girls are all in bed and I have rung the bell for the lights out.[6]

She then apologizes to her brother for giving such gloomy news, and suggests a possible answer to her plight:

> Be it and all things still, you seemed so anxious for me to stay in this school that I am sorry to show you the dark side of the picture in an assistant teacher's life in such a school as this.
> I am trying to take lessons in drawing and painting tho' I have but very little time, but I have some talent for it—I think and if—I can devote the vacation and the month of September to taking lessons perhaps I can teach it, and that would support me if—I could live with you . . .[7]

Later in April, a letter to her brother, George, reveals the anxiety and gloom which pervaded the land in those early months before the start of the Civil War:

> If our school is suspended, and I leave here where shall I go? If you men all go we women might as well be together in Columbia or somewhere. Write me what you intend and what you think I had best do if school is suspended on account of the war. I feel sad and anxious every day and I get very few letters. One of the professors in the college has just died whose wife is one of our teachers and an intimate friend of mine and that makes me more gloomy, . . .[8]

Mrs. Scott then describes the activities brought about by the impending war and reveals that determination and resignation which must have characterized many women in the South:

> . . . and to see the companies going to war one passed thro' today quite a large company. It looked like something very gay but I could not keep back the tears. When our company left—we came out to bid them good bye, you never saw such a time of weeping. I pray every day that those whom I love whose lives are precious to me be Christians & thus ready for either life or death. All Christians should pray to the Ruler of Nations, to be on our side and speedily restore peace. He who stilled the raging sea can quiet the waves of human passion, and soon bring order out of confusion. Give my best love to Mattie (her sister) tell her she must try to be a brave woman if her husband has to leave her for the

[6]**Ibid.**
[7]**Ibid.**
[8]Letter from Mrs. Sarah Jane Scott to her brother, George Duff, April 30, 1860.

> battlefield. I want us women all to learn to use the gun and the pistol well, and to ride well so that we can be ready if danger comes near home. God bless you all.[9]

In the last letter to be cited in this book Mrs. Scott ended on a note of hope and optimism:

> Mr. Clark is unwilling for me to give up my situation as I proposed & offers to increase my salary the first of January to forty-five dollars a month, that is ten dollars more in the month. (She had been receiving thirty-five dollars a month.) He insists that I can improve my education, and teach at the same time, says it will injure the school for me to give up and have another take my place as I propose, so I suppose I shall stay. . . . Mr. Clark proposes to increase my salary every year, since he says he is able to do it, is getting out of his embarrassments.[10]

Mrs. Scott then suggests that her brother come and live in Independence and take up his law practice in that community:

> . . . then I can live with you and keep my situation in this school, which is the first institution in the state and in which I can have a better position than anywhere in this state. You are so young the institution would perhaps offer you advantages particularly the Law department . . .[11]

Whether Mrs. Scott's brother came to Independence or not or whether he went off to war is another story as are the further adventures of Mrs. Sara Jane Scott, teacher.

---

[9]**Ibid.**

[10]Letter from Mrs. Sarah Jane Scott to her brother, George Duff, November 3, 1860.

[11]**Ibid.**

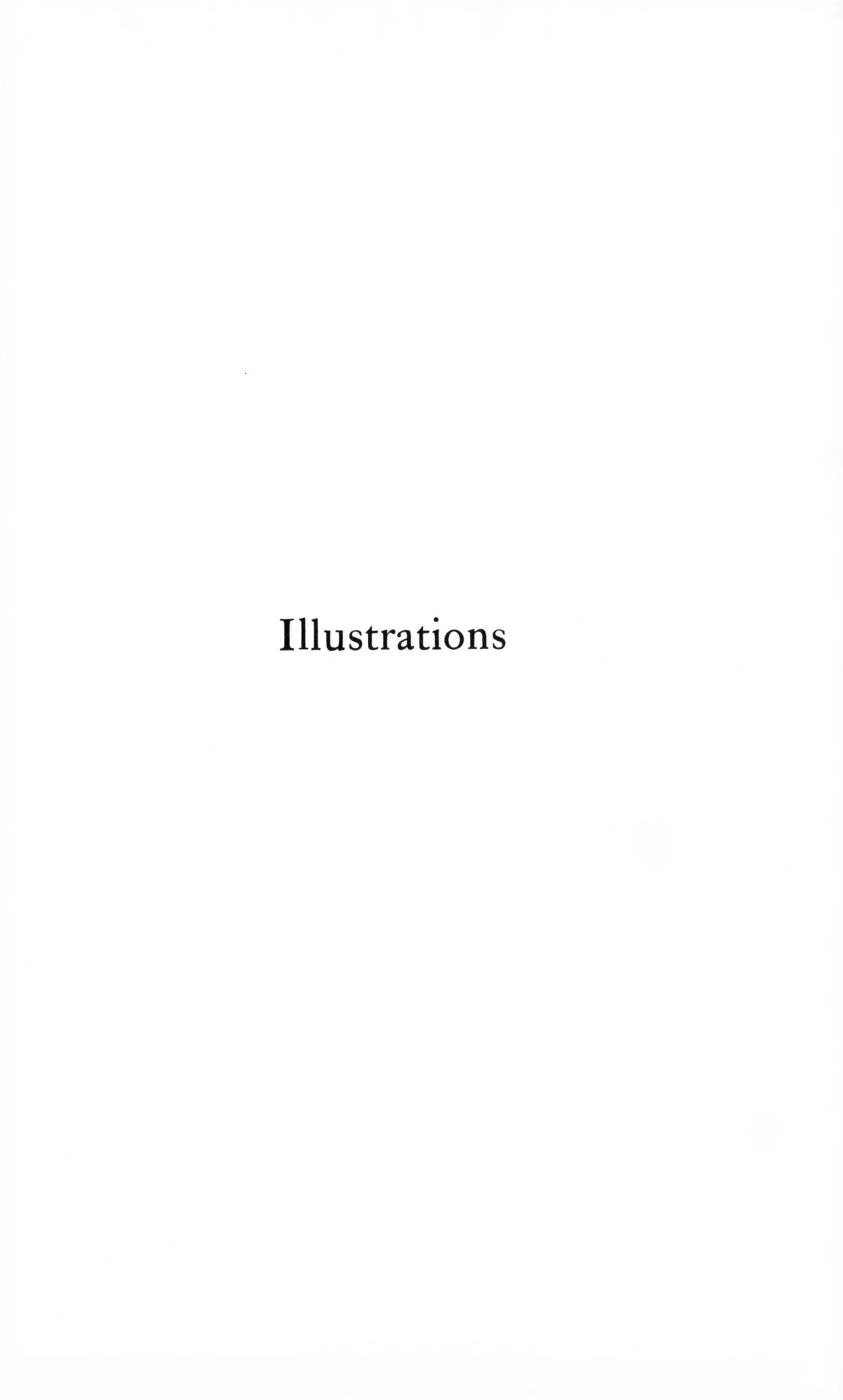

Illustrations

Map of Texas printed in 1855. Note Washington County outlined in black.

Anson Jones, President of the Republic of Texas when Baylor University received its charter in 1845.

Rev. Z. N. Morrell, outstanding Baptist leader and one of the first missionaries to come to Texas. He was an active member of the Education Society.

Statue erected by the State of Texas in honor of Judge R. E. B. Baylor. Located on the Waco campus of Baylor University.

ROBERT EMMETT BLEDSOE BAYLOR
1791 - 1873

FOUNDER OF BAYLOR UNIVERSITY
UNDER THE REPUBLIC OF TEXAS 1845
DONOR OF THE FIRST THOUSAND
DOLLARS TO THE INSTITUTION
PRESIDENT OF THE FIRST BOARD
OF TRUSTEES PROFESSOR IN
THE FIRST LAW FACULTY HE
EXEMPLIFIED IN HIS LIFE THE
MOTTO OF BAYLOR UNIVERSITY
PRO ECCLESIA PRO TEXANA

CONSTRUCTIVE STATESMAN

JUDGE BAYLOR
WAS A MEMBER OF THE
KENTUCKY LEGISLATURE
CONGRESSMAN FROM KENTUCKY
CONGRESSMAN FROM ALABAMA
UNITED STATES SENATOR FROM
ALABAMA HE SERVED
FIVE YEARS AS ASSOCIATE
JUSTICE OF THE SUPREME
COURT OF THE REPUBLIC
OF TEXAS TWENTY YEARS
AS DISTRICT JUDGE FOR
THE STATE COURTS AS
COMMANDER OF A COMPANY
IN THE WAR OF 1812
AND AS A SOLDIER IN
THE CREEK AND INDIAN
WAR MEXICAN WAR AND
THE TEXAS - INDIAN WAR

RELIGIOUS LEADER

JUDGE BAYLOR
ORGANIZED THE UNION
ASSOCIATION THE FIRST
BAPTIST ORGANIZATION IN
TEXAS PRESENTED THE
FIRST REPORT IN BEHALF
OF CHRISTIAN EDUCATION IN
TEXAS HE WAS THE FIRST
PRESIDENT OF THE TEXAS
EDUCATIONAL SOCIETY
SPONSOR OF A FREE PUBLIC
SCHOOL SYSTEM PREACHER
AND LAWYER HE PREACHED
THE FIRST SERMON AND HELD
THE FIRST COURT IN WACO
GIVING DIRECTION AND
DESTINY TO TEXAS BY
UPHOLDING THE LAW AND
PROCLAIMING THE GOSPEL

Inscriptions on the Baylor Statue

R. E. B. Baylor in later years

Monument erected to the memory of
William Tryon on the Baylor campus

WILLIAM MILTON TRYON
1809 - 1847

A FOUNDER OF BAYLOR

THE IDEA OF A BAPTIST
UNIVERSITY IN TEXAS
AND OF A BAPTIST STATE
CONVENTION ORIGINATED
WITH TRYON ACTIVE IN
THE ORGANIZATION OF THE
TEXAS BAPTIST EDUCATION
SOCIETY HE BECAME ITS
FIRST CORRESPONDING
SECRETARY AND THE FIRST
PERMANENT PRESIDENT OF
THE BOARD OF TRUSTEES
OF BAYLOR UNIVERSITY

EDUCATOR

MEMBER OF THE COMMITTEE
APPOINTED TO SECURE FROM
THE REPUBLIC OF TEXAS
A CHARTER FOR A BAPTIST
EDUCATIONAL INSTITUTION
TRYON REJECTED JUDGE
BAYLOR'S SUGGESTION THAT
THE SCHOOL BE NAMED TRYON
AND INTO THE APPLICATION
WROTE THE NAME BAYLOR

LEADER IN
CHURCH AND STATE

BORN IN NEW YORK CITY
AND EDUCATED AT MERCER
TRYON WAS THE SECOND
MISSIONARY SENT TO
TEXAS BY THE AMERICAN
BAPTIST HOME MISSION
SOCIETY HE SERVED AS
THE FIRST CORRESPONDING
SECRETARY OF THE TEXAS
BAPTIST HOME MISSION
SOCIETY, AS CHAPLAIN IN
THE CONGRESS OF THE
REPUBLIC OF TEXAS,
AND AS TREASURER OF THE
TEXAS LITERARY INSTITUTE

Inscriptions on the Tryon Monument

James Huckins

Monument erected in memory of James Huckins in Baylor campus

JAMES HUCKINS
1807 - 1863

A FOUNDER OF BAYLOR

HUCKINS RECOMMENDED
IN 1841 THE FORMATION
OF THE TEXAS BAPTIST
EDUCATION SOCIETY WITH
THE VIEW OF ESTABLISHING
AN ACADEMICAL AND
THEOLOGICAL INSTITUTION
HE WAS A MEMBER OF THE
BOARD OF MANAGERS OF THE
EDUCATION SOCIETY AND OF
THE BOARD OF TRUSTEES
OF BAYLOR UNIVERSITY

MISSIONARY - EDUCATOR

GENERAL AGENT OF THE
AMERICAN BAPTIST HOME
MISSION SOCIETY AND ITS
FIRST MISSIONARY TO
TEXAS, HUCKINS REACHED
GALVESTON IN 1840.
AS FINANCIAL AGENT OF
BAYLOR UNIVERSITY HE
RAISED $30,000 IN CASH,
NOTES, AND COMMODITIES.

LEADER IN
CHURCH AND STATE

BORN IN NEW HAMPSHIRE,
HUCKINS WAS EDUCATED AT
BROWN UNIVERSITY AND AT
ANDOVER THEOLOGICAL
SEMINARY. HE DEVOTED
TWENTY YEARS TO TEXAS
FOUNDED CHURCHES PREACHED
THE GOSPEL SERVED THREE
TIMES AS PRESIDENT OF THE
BAPTIST STATE CONVENTION
INITIATED CIVIC REFORM
AND FOSTERED EDUCATION

Inscriptions on the Huckins Monument

Rutersville College founded by the Methodists in 1840. Southwestern University at Georgetown traces its origin from this college.

Sketch of the main building used by Wesleyan College, a Methodist college chartered in 1844.

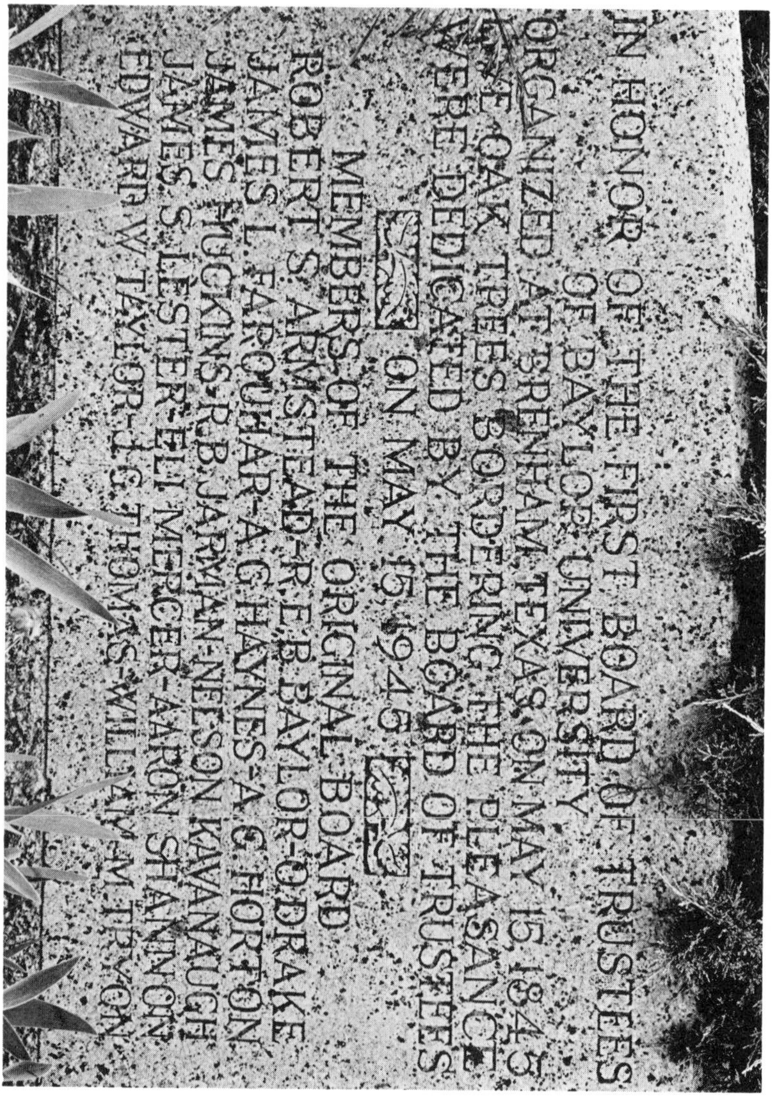

Monument erected on the Baylor campus in honor of the first Board of Trustees.

Rev. Joseph W. D. Creath. Creath not only contributed his time as a member of the Board of Trustees, he also gave $2,000 for the endowment of the Education Society and Baylor University. In his will he bequeathed his valuable theological library to the school.

Albert Galletan Haynes was a trustee and even by the standards of the day was quite wealthy. He boarded students at his home and contributed considerable sums of money to the school.

Rev. Robert H. Taliaferro, outstanding Baptist leader and as special correspondent of the *Texas Baptist,* wrote numerous articles about Baylor University.

Rev. George W. Baines, Sr.
Editor of the *Texas Baptist*
Baines was appointed a trustee in 1850. In 1861 he was elected President of Baylor University, and served in that capacity for two years.

The Texas Baptist.

DEVOTED ESPECIALLY TO THE RELIGIOUS AND EDUCATIONAL INTERESTS OF THE BAPTIST DENOMINATION IN TEXAS.

VOLUME I. ANDERSON, GRIMES COUNTY, TEXAS, APRIL 4, 1855. NUMBER XIV.

The *Texas Baptist* edited by George W. Baines, was the chief Baptist newspaper. Much news about Baylor during its early days at Independence appeared in the paper.

Mr. and Mrs. Henry Gillette. Gillette was the first teacher hired by the university. He was in charge of the preparatory school from 1846-1849.

Rev. Henry Lee Graves, first President of Baylor University and served in that capacity from 1847-1851.

Mr. and Mrs. R. C. Burleson in 1853

Rufus Columbus Burleson in later years

Horace Clark, principal of the Female Department from 1851-1861

Richard B. Burleson, brother of Rufus Burleson, taught in the Male Department from 1851-1860. Later he became Vice-President of Baylor University at Waco.

First faculty of the Male Department under Rufus Burleson. Left to right, top row: R. C. Burleson, R. B. Burleson, D. R. Wallace; bottom row, left to right, O. H. Leland, J. L. Smith, G. W. Willric.

A. S. Lipscomb, trustee and part-time professor in the law school from 1851-1855, later became a judge of the first Texas Supreme Court.

Royal T. Wheeler, law professor at Baylor University from 1857 to 1858. Later he established his own law school at Brenham and became a part of the Burleson-Clark controversy. Wheeler went on to become a justice of the first Texas Supreme Court.

Sam Houston, for a time, lived near Baylor University and was a frequent guest speaker. He, also, allowed the students at the institution to use his extensive library.

Sketch of the first building used by Baylor University, from the sketchbook of Mrs. Georgia Burleson.

Model of the first building used by Baylor University. In the first five years, this was the only building used by both the boys and girls of the school. In 1851 the male department moved to a stone building on Allen Hill and left the old wooden structure for the female department. This building was used by the girls until about 1857.

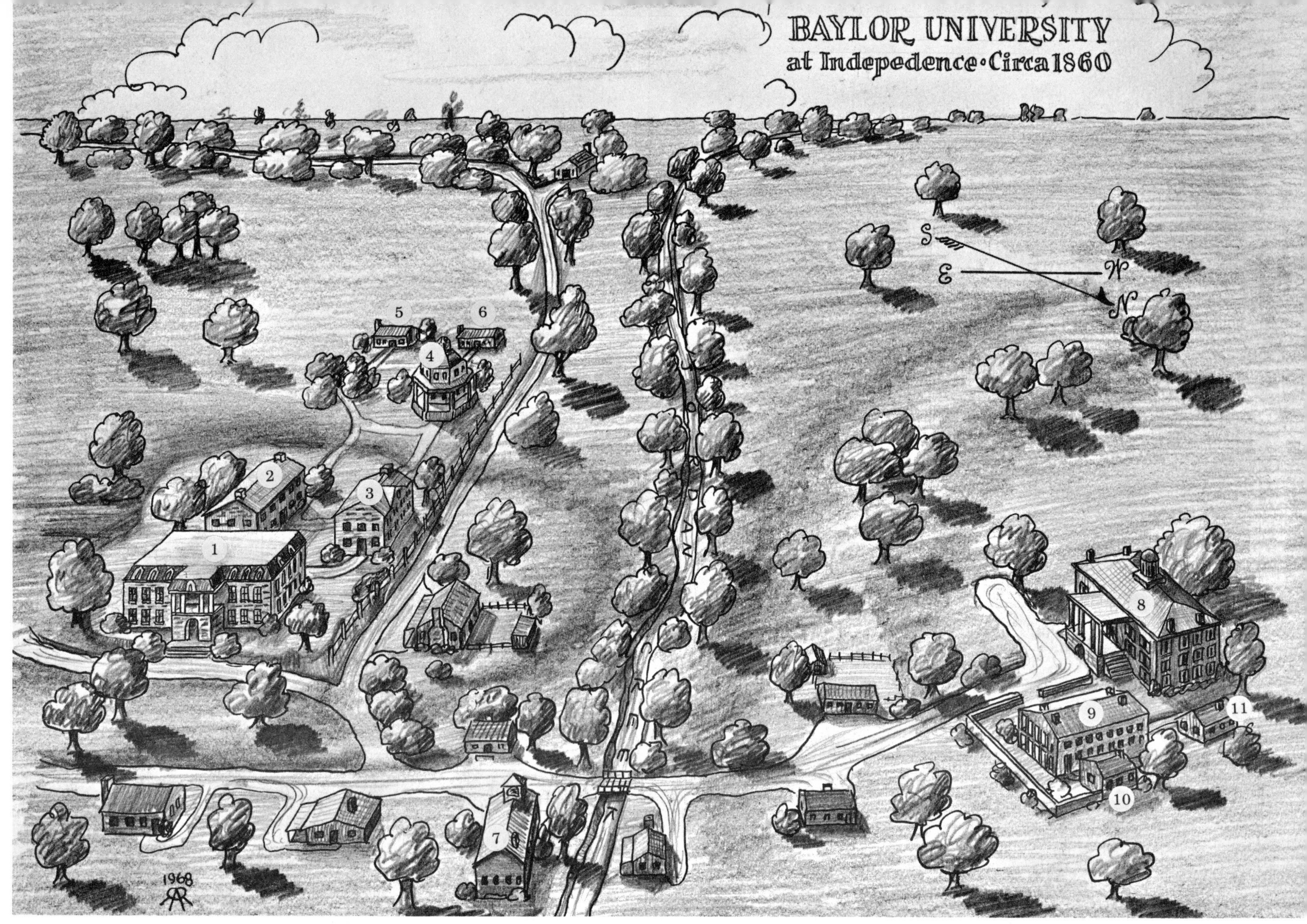

MALE CAMPUS

1. Tryon Hall
2. First Stone Building
3. Wing Building
4. Octagon House
5. Dormitory
6. Dormitory
7. Independence Baptist Church

FEMALE CAMPUS

8. College Edifice
9. Dormitory
10. Kitchen
11. Dining Hall

The first stone building erected on Allen Hill. Occupied by Burleson and the Male Department in 1851.

Model of the Male Department campus as it appeared about 1860.

1. Tryon Hall, planned as the main building, was never completely finished or used.
2. The first stone building on the site, first used by the male department in 1851.
3. Second stone "Wing Building" constructed in 1859-1860.
4. The Octagon House built by Burleson served as the President's Mansion and a boarding house.
5. & 6. Small two-room dormitories.

Model of the Female Campus

1. College Edifice
2. Boarding House
3. Dining Hall
4. Kitchen
5. Clark's Residence

Stones from Tryon Hall, main building of the male department at Independence, now on the Baylor campus at Waco.

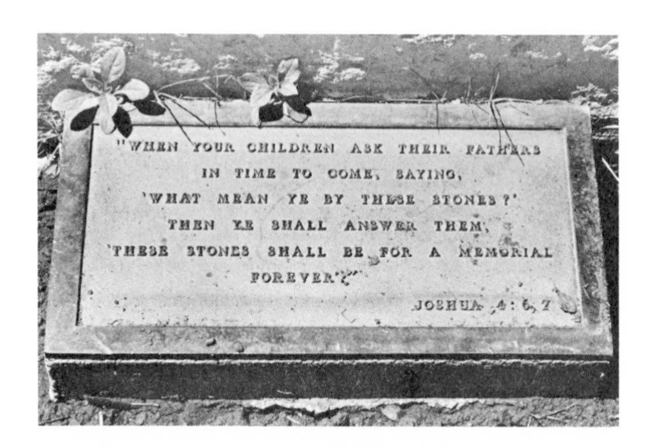

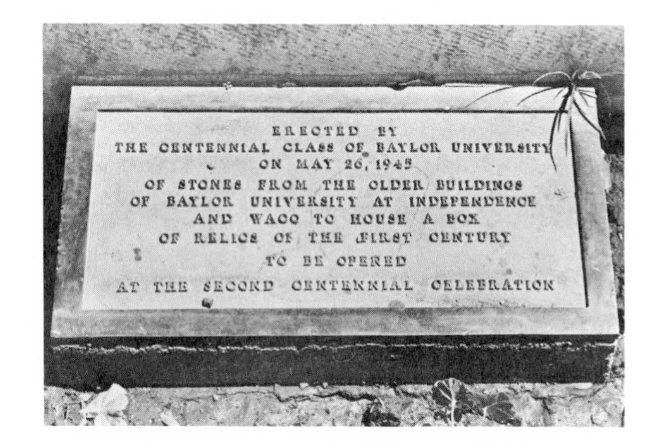

Bronze plaques at the foot of the Tryon column

Columns of the College Edifice, main building of the female department, as they appear today.

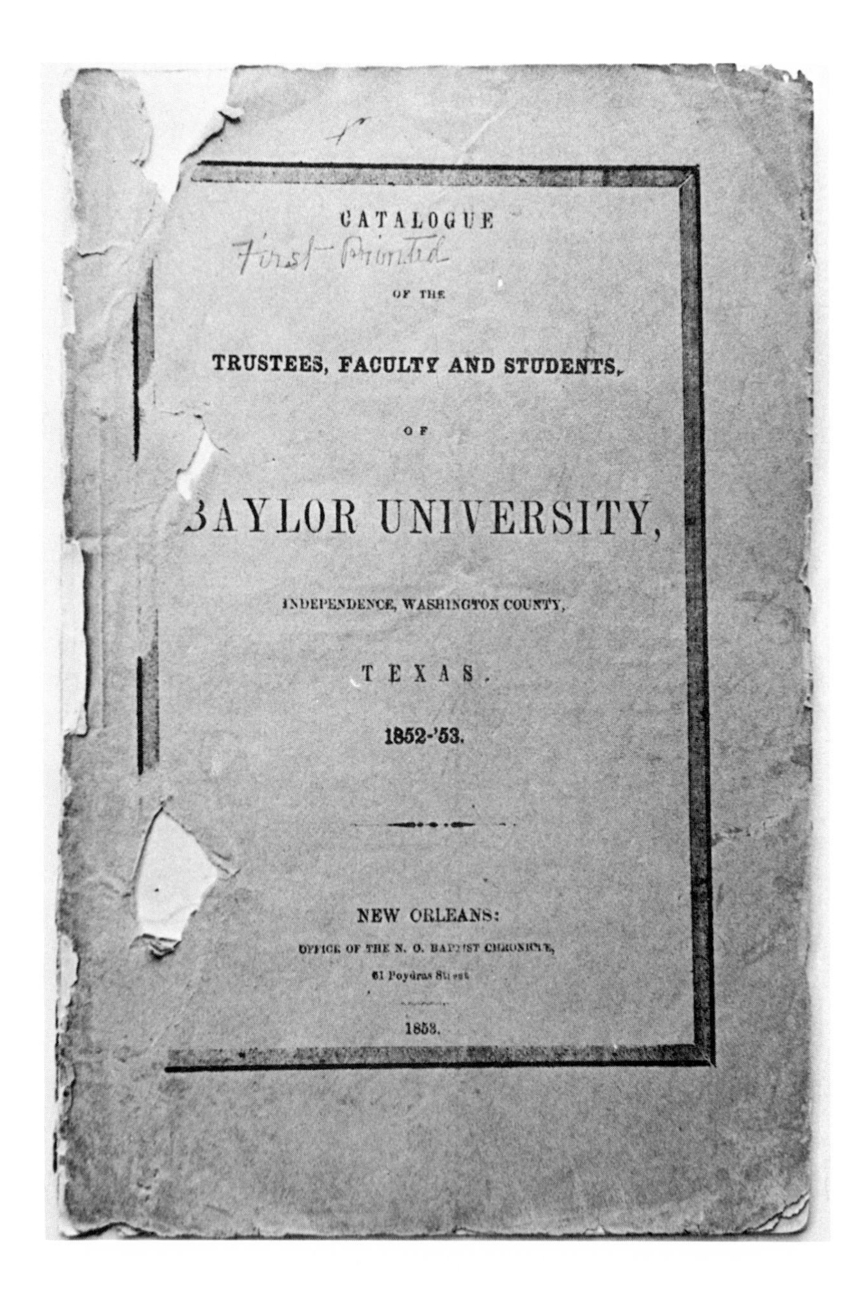

CATALOGUE

First Printed

OF THE

TRUSTEES, FACULTY AND STUDENTS,

OF

BAYLOR UNIVERSITY,

INDEPENDENCE, WASHINGTON COUNTY,

TEXAS.

1852-'53.

NEW ORLEANS:

OFFICE OF THE N. O. BAPTIST CHRONICLE,

61 Poydras Street

1853.

The first printed catalogue of Baylor University

CATALOGUE

OF THE

TRUSTEES, FACULTY

AND

STUDENTS

OF

Baylor University.

FEMALE

Department.

INDEPENDENCE, TEXAS.

For the Year 1857.

PRINTED AT THE GALVESTON 'NEWS' BOOK AND JOB ESTABLISHMENT.

1857.

First known printed catalogue of the Female Department

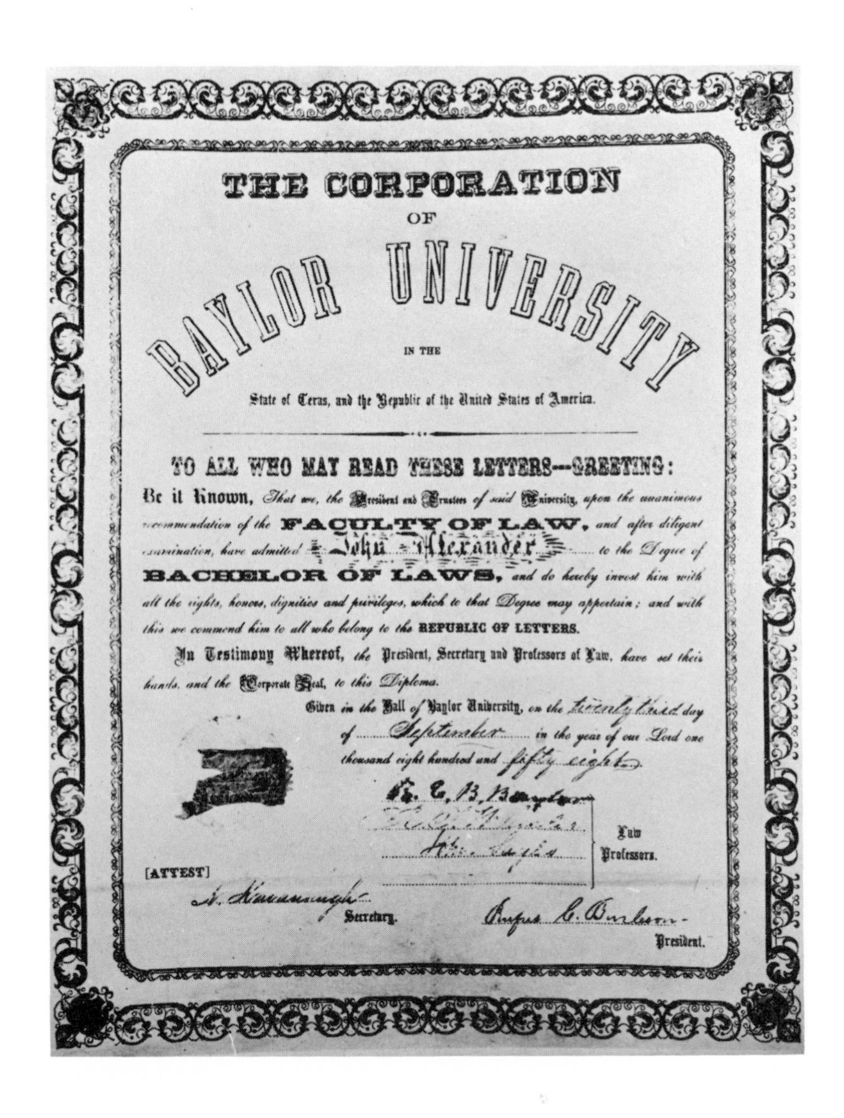

THE CORPORATION
OF
BAYLOR UNIVERSITY
IN THE
State of Texas, and the Republic of the United States of America.

TO ALL WHO MAY READ THESE LETTERS---GREETING:

Be it Known, *That we, the* President and Trustees *of said* University, *upon the unanimous recommendation of the* FACULTY OF LAW, *and after diligent examination, have admitted* John Alexander *to the Degree of* BACHELOR OF LAWS, *and do hereby invest him with all the rights, honors, dignities and privileges, which to that Degree may appertain; and with this we commend him to all who belong to the* REPUBLIC OF LETTERS.

In Testimony Whereof, *the* President, Secretary and Professors of Law, *have set their hands, and the* Corporate Seal, *to this Diploma.*

Given *in the* Hall *of* Baylor University, *on the* twenty third *day of* September *in the year of our Lord one thousand eight hundred and* fifty eight.

[illegible] } Law Professors.

[ATTEST]

[illegible]
Secretary.

Rufus C. Burleson
President.

Degree awarded by Baylor University in 1858

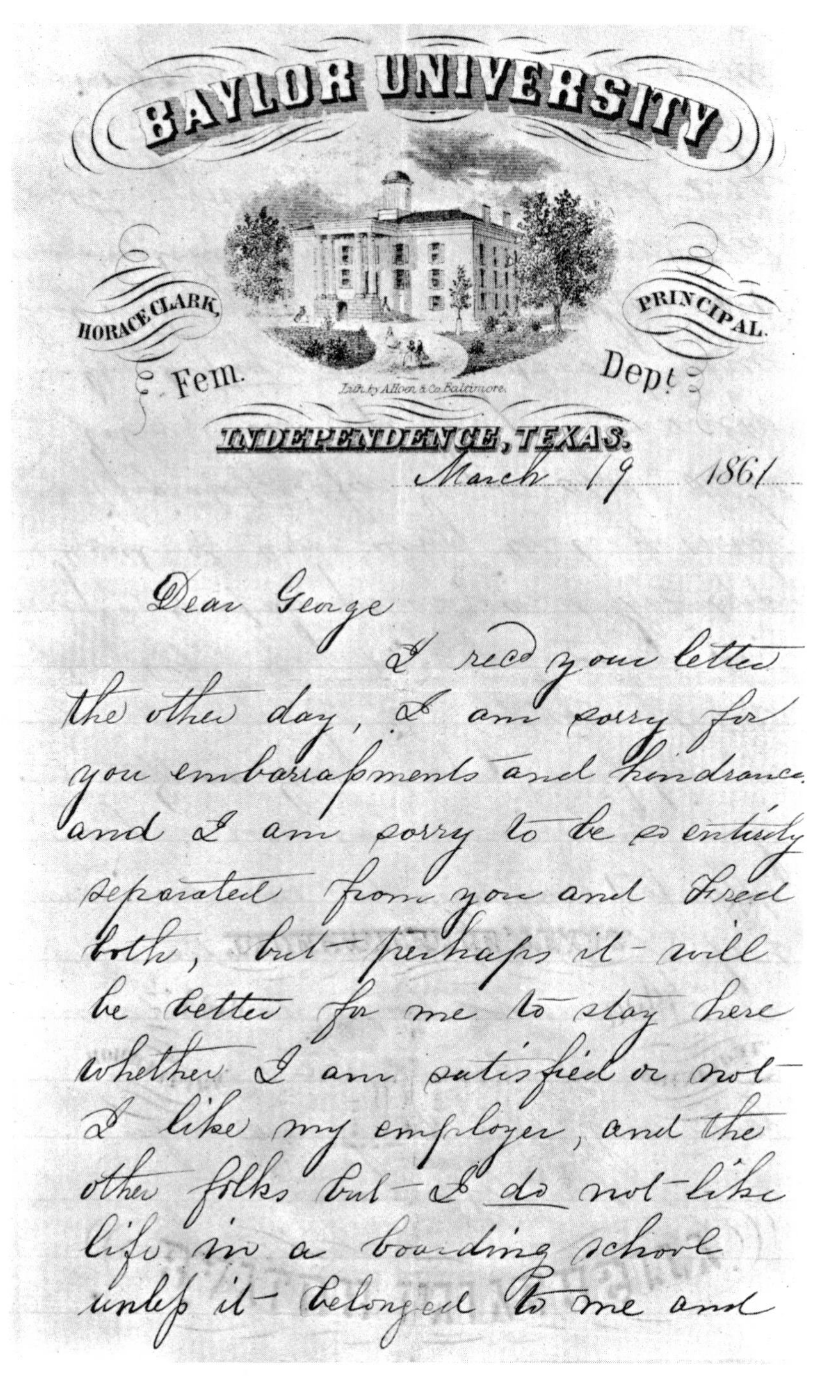

BAYLOR UNIVERSITY

HORACE CLARK, PRINCIPAL.

Fem. Dept.

Lith. by A. Hoen & Co. Baltimore.

INDEPENDENCE, TEXAS. March 19 1861

Dear George

I recd your letter the other day, I am sorry for you embarrassments and hindrances and I am sorry to be so entirely separated from you and Fred both, but perhaps it will be better for me to stay here whether I am satisfied or not I like my employer, and the other folks but I do not like life in a boarding school unless it belonged to me and

Letter from Mrs. Sarah Jane Scott, teacher in the female department, showing Baylor University letterhead.

Bibliography

UNPUBLISHED MATERIALS

Collections

Baylor Family Papers. Texas Collection, Baylor University

Baylor University at Independence Collection. Texas Collection, Baylor University.

Erisophian Society Papers. Texas Collection, Baylor University.

George W. Baines Papers. Texas Collection, Baylor University.

Henry Graves Papers. Texas Collection, Baylor University.

Horace Clark Papers. Texas Collection, Baylor University.

Philomathesian Society Papers. Texas Collection, Baylor University.

Rufus C. Burleson Papers. Texas Collection, Baylor University.

Richard B. Burleson Papers. Texas Collection, Baylor University.

Records

Hosea Garrett Subscription Book. Texas Collection, Baylor University.

Minutes of the Board of Trustees of Baylor University at Independence. 1845-1887. Texas Collection, Baylor University.

Minutes of the Board of Trustees of Waco University and Classical School. 1861-1887. Texas Collection, Baylor University.

Theses, Themes

Duncan, Frances Higginbotham. "The Life and Times of R. E. B. Baylor 1793-1846." Unpublished Master's thesis, History Department, Baylor University, 1954.

Gambrell, Herbert. "The Early Baylor University 1841-1861." Unpublished Master's thesis, History Department, Southern Methodist University, 1924.

Grusendorf, Arthur August. "The Baptists and Education in Washington County, 1845-1875." Unpublished theme, Texas Collection, Baylor University, n.d.

PUBLISHED MATERIALS

Books

Benedict, David. *A General History of the Baptist Denomination in America and Other Parts.* New York: Lewis Colby and Company, 1848.

Carl, Prince of Solms-Braunfels. *Texas 1844-1845.* Houston: The Anson Jones Press, 1936.

Carroll, J. M. *A History of Texas Baptists.* Dallas: Baptist Standard Publishing Co., 1923.

Dawson, Joseph Martin. *A Century with Texas Baptists.* Nashville: Broadman Press, 1947.

Dietrich, Wilfred O. *The Blazing Story of Washington County.* Brenham: Banner Press, 1950.

Eby, Fredrick. *The Development of Education in Texas.* New York: The Macmillan Company, 1925.

Haynes, Harry. *The Life and Writings of Rufus C. Burleson.* Compiled and published by Georgia J. Burleson, 1901.

Lane, J. J. *History of Education in Texas.* Washington: Government Printing Office, 1903.

Laws of the Republic of Texas Passed at the Session of the 5th Congress. Houston: The Republic of Texas, 1841.

Link, J. B. (ed.). *Texas Historical and Biographical Magazine,* Vol. I. Austin: 1891.

Morrell, Z. N. *Fruits and Flowers from the Wilderness of 36 Years in Texas.* Houston: Gould and Lincoln, 1872.

Nail, Olin W. (ed.). *Texas Methodist Centennial Yearbook.* Elgin, Texas: 1934.

Private and Denominational Efforts. Vol. IV of *A Documentary History of Education in the South Before 1860.* Edited by J. Edgar Knight. Chapel Hill: University of North Carolina Press, 1933.

Ray, Worth S. *Austin Colony Pioneers.* Austin: 1949.

Riley, B. F. *History of the Baptists in Texas.* Dallas: B. F. Riley, 1907.

Schmidt, Charles F. *History of Washington County.* San Antonio: Naylor Co., 1949.

Walker, James L. *History of the Waco Baptist Association of Texas.* Waco: Bryne-Hill Printing House, 1897.

Articles

Crane, R. C. "Tryon Hall," *Baylor Monthly,* V (April, 1929), 12.

Haynes, Harry. "Dr. Rufus C. Burleson," *Southwestern Historical Review,* V (July, 1901), 49-60.

Catalogues, Annuals

Baptist State Convention. *Texas Baptist Annals,* 1852-1872.

Baylor University. *Catalogues,* 1851-1885.

Pamphlets

Baptist State Convention of Texas. *Organization Proceedings.* Anderson County, Texas: 1848.

Baylor University, *Laws of Baylor University.* Austin: 1854.

Independence Baptist Church. *Covenant and Articles of Faith.* Independence: c. 1899.

Newspapers

Baylor Aegis, July, 1881.

South-Western Baptist Chronicle (New Orleans, Louisiana). 1848-1849.

Telegraph and Texas Register (Houston, Texas). November 19, 1845.

Texas Baptist (Anderson, Texas). 1855-1860.

Texas Baptist Herald (Houston, Texas). 1857-1859.

Washington-American (Washington, Texas). 1855-1857.

Index

— G —

— H —

— I —

— J —

— K —

— L —

— Mc —

— M —